About Walte_ _____ _

"One of the great blessings God has granted me in my life is the opportunity to have co-ministered with [Walter Bradley] among faculty and students on university campuses across the US and beyond."

—Hugh Ross, PhD, Reasons to Believe

"Walter Bradley is one of the most remarkable Christian scholars I've ever known."

—Robert B. Sloan, DTh,
president of Houston Baptist University

"I learned from Walter that you can live out loud as a Christian academic."

—Dr. Lawrence Murphy Smith, CPA

"Walter Bradley and his wife, Ann, helped my husband, Blake, and me through the most beautiful and most painful journey in our lives."

—Elisa Teipel, PhD, Essentium, Inc.

"Walter was instrumental in helping me understand that my gifts and talents as an engineer could be used to serve the poor and marginalized."

—Professor Brian Thomas,
executive director of Baylor University
Justice and Mercy Energy Services

"Professor Walter Bradley fearlessly led the charge for faculty to unabashedly stand up for their faith on campuses."

—James M. Tour, PhD, Rice University

"Knowing and being mentored by Walter Bradley has been one of God's greatest blessings."

—John F. Walkup, PhD, Horn Professor,
Texas Tech University (retired)

For a Greater Purpose

THE LIFE AND LEGACY OF
WALTER BRADLEY

For a Greater Purpose

THE LIFE AND LEGACY OF *WALTER BRADLEY*

ROBERT J. MARKS II
WILLIAM A. DEMBSKI

FOREWORD BY J.P. MORELAND

NASHVILLE, TENNESSEE

Erasmus
P R E S S

An imprint of Influence Publishers
A division of Education Access, LLC
www.influencepublishers.com

First edition.

Printed in the United States of America

ISBN: 978-1-64542-713-1 (trade paper)
ISBN: 978-1-64542-714-8 (e-book)
ISBN: 978-1-64542-715-5 (audiobook)

Cover design by Derek Thornton, Notch Design
Cover photography copyright © Laszlo Bencze

Dedication

To all who are making the world a better place because
they know Walter and Ann Bradley.

Contents

Foreword

I had never suffered a concussion in my life, but there I was, lying on my back in the middle of a field, experiencing a twilight wooziness that made me want to faint. Suddenly I noticed a hand enter my cloudy field of vision and a voice asked me how many fingers he was holding up. "Three," I said, and as I did, I began to come out of it and saw to whom the hand belonged: Butch (we used to call him that) Bradley!

It was October 1970. That June I graduated from college, joined the staff of Campus Crusade for Christ (now known as Cru), and was assigned to the University of Colorado in Boulder three and a half days a week and to the Colorado School of Mines in Golden a day and a half a week. Butch was on associate staff with Crusade and started and directed the Crusade movement at Mines. I would drive to Golden every Sunday afternoon, stay with the Bradleys, minister all day Monday, then drive back to Boulder. This went on for two years, and I got to know the Bradleys, especially Butch, very well.

Back to the concussion. Butch had started a Campus Crusade intramural football team, and we won all our games but one—the one in which I got the concussion. I reached down to grab a guy's flag and accidentally got kneed in the head. Butch played both offense and defense on the team, and he was aggressive, passionate, and really good. He was somewhat of a legend at the time (for reasons that will become evident as you read this book), but his willingness to get down and dirty with the Crusade students and me was one of the things I've always loved about him.

Walter is an absolutely extraordinary human being manifested in a down-to-earth, "ordinary" kind of personality. As I write this, I've known

Walter for fifty years, and he has always had a humble servant's heart in spite of his stunning accomplishments and the amazing person he has become.

In my fifty-two years as a Jesus-follower, a very select group of four outstanding Christians have by far had the greatest impact on my Christian life (besides my wife and a few very close friends): Bill Bright (founder of Campus Crusade), Howard Hendricks (professor at Dallas Theological Seminary), Dallas Willard (personal friend and dissertation mentor at the University of Southern California), and Walter Bradley. In the pages to follow, as we celebrate and honor Walter's life, it will become evident why I regard him so highly. But for now I want to list some of the things about Walter that make me love and admire him so much.

1. *Zeal and passion for God.* Walter constantly shares the gospel with others and is deeply committed to evangelism, discipleship, and the aggressive pursuit of Jesus and His kingdom. Walter has always been zealous for promoting a rational Christian faith that is based on evidence and argument.

2. *Honest, straight-shooting seeker of truth; a man of integrity.* In all the years I've known Butch, what you see is what you get with him. He is comfortable in his own skin and does not try to be what he is not; there is not a fake or pretentious bone in his body (except when he's trying to tell me how to do philosophy!). So many times I've seen him graciously call an atheist's bluff and say frankly that his objection is really pretty weak. On the other hand, Walter always wants to know if his view on something or his case for it is wrong, so he would approach naturalists on the faculty with him or in other contexts to seek feedback on his lectures or writings. He isn't the sort of Christian who hides from others. He is an open book who seeks to be honest regarding his Christianity. Walter is quite simply a man of integrity, the exact opposite of a phony or pretender. He isn't particularly impressed with himself, but he is *really* impressed with Jesus!

3. *Steady and reliable.* If a situation arose and everyone was in panic mode, Walter could always be counted on to keep his cool. He is

unflappable. If Butch is living for something or has set a worthy goal, nothing can stop him until the goal is reached. He is immovable and just keeps going. And if he gives you his word, he keeps it.

4. *Life of the mind.* Walter has always believed in, nurtured, and promoted the life of the mind as central for the life of the disciple of Jesus. He is constantly reading, growing, and asking questions. If he doesn't know something, he keeps digging until he does.

Walter has always been a role model for these values and many more. In the pages to follow, you will enter into his story as the history of his life unfolds. But this is no mere biography, as wonderful as his life has been. Rather, it is a story meant to inspire the reader to strive for more in his or her Christian life and to see how a role model beloved by so many went about his own life. So enjoy, but learn and grow.

J. P. Moreland

Preface

When the office of a retiring colleague was cleaned out in my engineering department at Baylor, boxes of papers and personal effects were placed in the hall outside the office door. To assure the boxes would be removed by the night cleaning staff, the word *Trash* was written loudly on a sheet of paper and taped to the largest box. What a sad metaphor for a professor's career, indeed for any career.

Walter Bradley's life and career, by contrast, is unforgettable. His legacy has been established both inside and outside his day job as a university professor. The impact of his life both professionally and as a lay ambassador for Christ is widespread and enduring. Many Christians aspire to a heritage like this. Yet ironically, such a goal cannot be achieved by making it a goal. It comes indirectly from dedicated hard work, bold decisions, and living a life selflessly motivated by a mission greater than self.

Like blind men with an elephant, most who have been impacted by Walter do not know the full extent of who he is or the many ways he and his wife, Ann, motivated by their faith in Jesus Christ, are leaving this world a better place.

Today's heroes are typically politicians, sports figures, pop musicians, and movie stars whose claim to fame is calling attention to themselves rather than fulfilling a higher calling of service to others. Our world needs heroes whose lives have positively and permanently impacted others. If you don't know Walter Bradley yet, our ardent hope is that he will be such a hero to you after reading this book.

By way of acknowledgment, we want to thank all the people who directly or indirectly helped bring this book to fruition—many of your names appear in these pages for the stories and insights you shared with us about Walter and Ann.

Robert J. Marks II
William A. Dembski

PART ONE

Charting a Path

1943–1976

Imagine a room full of people who all know Dr. Walter Bradley.

One of them says, "Dr. Bradley is one of the most honored and respected engineering professors in academia today."

"Really?" says another. "I know him as a fearless and articulate Christian apologist."

"To me Dr. Bradley is one of the most effective advocates of intelligent design in the past thirty years," says a third.

"He has been a kind and compassionate confidante for thousands of students for longer than that," declares a fourth.

"Are we talking about the same Walter Bradley?" asks a fifth. "I've seen the Dr. Bradley I know hand a hot-shot lawyer his own backside on a platter as an expert witness in the courtroom."

The comments continue.

"I thought he was best known for his research for NASA and aircraft designers on high-performance materials for spacecraft and military jets."

"He's the best Bible teacher I ever had."

"He and his wife, Ann, have planted the seeds of Christian outreach on college campuses across the country."

"He has transformed the lives of thousands of people in the developing world with engineering projects that make their communities safer, more comfortable, and more prosperous."

"You can always tell a Texan, but you can't tell him much."

As those who know him well can attest, all of these descriptions of Walter Bradley are true. He is at the same time a great academician and scientist and a great Christian leader and humanitarian.

But before he was any of these, he was a young graduate student trying to figure out what to do with his life.

CHAPTER 1

Five Minutes on Wednesday

It seemed like a good idea at the time to Walter "Butch" Bradley.
Sitting at the kitchen table of their campus apartment going over the
plan with his wife, Ann, not only did they believe it was a solid course of
action, it felt like the right thing to do. Butch was a young man constantly
in motion. For him, turning ideas into action was as natural as day following night. Once he and Ann had made their decision, he was eager to
move ahead.

The time was right for him to tell his students that the reason he
treated them with care and respect was that he was a follower of Christ.

Butch was teaching an undergraduate business calculus class to sup-
plement his National Science Foundation fellowship stipend, which paid
all of his school and living expenses, and Ann's modest public school
teaching income while he was pursuing a doctorate at the University of
Texas. While some of his college classmates struggled to keep up with
their assignments, Bradley maintained a 4.0 GPA to be sure that he kept
his fellowship. Earning a doctorate in materials science was a tall order,
but Butch was used to hard work. He had had a job since he was eleven
years old, and as an undergraduate he'd juggled a twenty-hour workweek
and eighteen hours of classes every semester.

Butch worked partly out of necessity. His mother had a good job and
gave him and his sister everything they needed growing up, but there was
no money to pay for college. Still, Virginia Bradley drilled into her son

that he was absolutely going to get a degree and that was what he'd been doing for the last five years. He had already worked to pay his way through his BS degree in engineering at the University of Texas and was continuing to work to complete his doctorate. He was at UT for both its excellent reputation in engineering and its accessibility. In-state tuition was fifty dollars per semester. And the campus was close enough to Butch's home in Corpus Christi, two hundred miles to the southeast on the Gulf Coast, that he could hitchhike back and forth.

The other reason Butch worked so hard was that he was born to work. He is a doer, an achiever, a man of action who draws genuine pleasure out of setting goals and reaching them. He considers it a blessing that he likes to work and that he had such a strong work ethic in college. The grand plan was to add an MBA to his credentials as well, then start up the career ladder at a major high-tech corporation. Butch wanted to be a CEO one day. But first he had to finish his doctoral degree.

Teaching came naturally to Butch. He liked to share what he knew and was good at explaining things. His undergrad business calculus students were only a few years younger than he was, but they liked their instructor. Kind, clear, confident—Butch was all those things from his first day in front of a class. Though he was young, Butch's maturity, expertise, and easygoing manner quickly won his students' respect.

Before that day in the kitchen with Ann, Butch never thought of teaching as an excellent opportunity to have a Christian influence. Such influence seemed completely absent on campus. If there were no visible committed Christian professors on the faculty, maybe it was a sign that Christians were deemed intellectually suspect in the academic world. How could they be taken seriously—especially the scientists—if they believed all that Jesus stuff? On the question of a teaching career, Bradley later wrote, "The idea had never occurred to me because in the seventy-five classes I took at the University of Texas, I had not one professor who self-identified as a Christian."

But after praying about it, Butch and Ann realized that teaching as a graduate student gave Butch the ideal opportunity to test the waters on the matter of revealing his faith to academia. The plan, which seemed so perfect as they refined it at their kitchen table, was that he would take five minutes one day at the end of his freshman business calculus class to share some personal biographical details about himself. The last, but most important, fact he wanted them to know was that he was a follower of Jesus Christ. By that he did not simply mean that he went to church, but that his relationship with Jesus was the foundation of his entire life. He hoped his students would see that his faith made a difference in how he treated them in class.

He was aware that if he got serious pushback, or if somebody complained to the administration, he might get called in by the department head to explain why he was talking about religion during class at a state university. Worst case, he might not be invited back to teach next semester, which meant he would have to find another part-time job his last year in graduate school. But Ann and Butch were confident his long-term professional prospects wouldn't be jeopardized since he had no plans whatsoever to teach for a living.

Though faculty members steered clear of any mention of religious preferences, Butch knew there was a Christian presence on the University of Texas campus. The first he had heard of it was near the end of his freshman year in 1962. That spring he saw a poster advertising an appearance by Dr. Bill Bright to speak to the UT chapter of Campus Crusade for Christ. It was providential that although Butch had never heard of Bill Bright or Campus Crusade, he went to the meeting. Bright "gave one of the best talks I ever heard," Butch said. "And it gave me the chance to meet one of the great Christians of our time who became one of the most important Christians of the twentieth century and the greatest Christian influence in my life."

Butch considers that first encounter with Bill Bright a seminal moment in his faith journey. Had it not been for that meeting, Butch might never have realized the possibility of having a close personal relationship with Jesus and sharing his faith with others. Though his undergraduate workload continued to keep him busy, over the next several years Butch went to occasional CCC weekly meetings or conferences. "I could have made time to do more if I'd had a bigger vision," he later recalled. At these events he "learned and grew in ways that were important. Campus Crusade kept me from remaining a spiritual baby for my whole life."

Butch began to feel the influence of his faith not only on Sundays in church but every day in every part of his character. His faith should be something his students were interested in. How could they not be curious?

As Butch explained, "My plan was to make a special effort to get to know my students for the first half of the semester by demonstrating Christian love toward them. Then I would take a few minutes at the end of one of my classes about mid-semester to share briefly more about myself, including a brief Christian testimony." After a forty-five-minute lecture, he planned to present his "five-minute personal biographical sketch that emphasized that the most important thing to know about me was that I was a follower of Jesus Christ and that I hoped that they would see that it made a difference in how I treated them."

Butch and Ann decided he would speak to his students that Wednesday. But as the time approached, he reconsidered the risk to his teaching position and the essential income it brought in. Would a simple statement of faith bring down the curtain on future teaching opportunities, which he needed to support his family while he finished his degree?

Butch picked up the story: "My wife and I prayed that Wednesday morning and I went to school excited and nervous." He gave his forty-five-minute lecture perfectly, but then, standing in front of the class, poised to continue, he realized he couldn't follow through with his plan. "I chickened out," he admitted, "afraid of what my students might think of me or, worse yet, say to the department head."

Butch continued, "I rationalized that Friday would be a better time so that they could have an extra day to think about it and/or get over it during the weekend." He reported his failure to Ann and promised himself he'd follow through the next class. But on Friday he repeated the same pattern: a perfect forty-five-minute lecture, another self-described "panic attack," and another class dismissal five minutes early.

The following Monday was an opportunity for a fresh start. But Butch chickened out a third time. And the time after that.

"For twenty-two shameful classes in a row I repeated this painful process," Bradley said, "beginning to despair that I could ever win this fierce spiritual battle." At long last, on the last day of class, he held on to his resolve. "Before handing out my final exams," he said, "I was finally able to take five minutes to briefly share my faith with my students, comforted with the knowledge that I would probably not likely see them again on the large UT campus."

Butch didn't take advantage of his position to preach or proselytize. He wasn't delivering a sales pitch, just a personal statement of fact. If any of them had questions, he would be glad to talk with them later. If they had objections, they would soon disappear into the sea of thirty thousand students on campus and wouldn't likely cross paths with him again. That first time did not receive much of a reaction. His students were all focused on their final exams and then on celebrating the end of the term. Butch waited a few days to see if any of them complained to the administration. Evidently no one did because he heard no more about it.

Butch's short presentation that day was a key moment in his professional and spiritual life: those five minutes had an outsized impact on all the days and decades that followed. "For my students," Bradley said, "it was probably an odd but insignificant non-event, but for me it was breaking a very important faith barrier. Never again would publicly identifying myself as a follower of Jesus to my students be so difficult! I had finally taken my first step in my journey toward becoming the Christian professor that God was calling me to be."

Once the ice was broken, talking about his Christian faith seemed like the most natural thing in the world to Butch. The next time it was significantly easier. And it produced dramatic results.

"The next semester," Butch later wrote, "I was able to share with my class in the middle of the semester (and on my first try) that I was a follower of Jesus. A student rushed up after the class anxious to talk. He had been contemplating suicide that very day! My brief comments pointed him to the God of hope and the real cure for his depression. I was elated as I was able to help this student, but I never would have connected with him without sharing with my class that I had become a follower of Jesus Christ as a college student and inviting any student who wanted to know more to talk to me outside of class."

At the same time Butch was delivering short affirmations of his spiritual journey to his classes, his own faith was strengthening and developing. However, he sensed a stagnation or hesitancy. Deep down, if he was honest with himself, he knew the reason why. He was coming to a fork in the road in his spiritual walk, which he realized forced him "to come to terms with the question of whether I was going to seek to know and do God's plan for my life, or continue with my own plan to become president of a large technical company."

Butch had an officemate in graduate school who wasn't a Christian when they met. Over time, after hearing Christian speakers and thinking about spiritual matters, he became a follower of Jesus with Ann's and Butch's encouragement. After the friend changed majors, Butch saw him less often.

One night Butch and Ann invited this fellow student to their apartment between Christmas and New Year's. The friend had just been to a Christmas conference sponsored by Campus Crusade for Christ. In the year and a half since they had been in regular contact, he had grown rapidly in his faith. Butch recalled him being "filled with joy and sense of purpose that comes when people really allow God to direct them."

Butch believed his own Christian growth had stalled "because I had quit saying yes." By contrast, their friend that evening "was just walking on clouds." Butch realized "God wanted me to trust Him with my future and I was afraid that would mean giving up science and the corporate world."

As Butch recalled, "Our friend left and Ann and I looked at each other and said it was ironic that we introduced him to Christ, and now he was already so far down the road from where we were. That meant we had to stop digging in our heels and instead trust that God's plan for our lives will surely be better than our own."

The year Butch first told his students he was a Christian was a time when he was at a crossroad of determining what he was going to do with his life. On one hand, he wanted to be whatever God wanted him to be. On the other hand, he had specific ideas about what he was good at, what he liked to do, and what sort of professional career those abilities pointed him toward. He knew he wanted a career involving math and science and remained wary of what God might have in store that was at odds with Butch's own vision for his future.

He admitted to himself that he was worried: "If I get really serious about my relationship with God, He's going to want me to put all my cards on the table. I really want to do something in math and science, and I can't use them if I'm being a missionary. At the time I wasn't sure God's way was better than mine. How stupid is that?!"

Toward the end of graduate school, Butch found the faith to trust God to do what was best for him. As he put it, "God, if it's Your plan for me to be a missionary in darkest Africa, You will change my heart and I will want to be a missionary in darkest Africa."

Summarizing that crucial stage of his spiritual journey, Butch explained, "I came to embrace this view of life through a three-year struggle from my junior year in college until my second year in graduate school. I wanted to have a close relationship with God, but I was afraid to give God my plans for my life and accept His *better* plans. I was afraid that God would call me to be a missionary or a minister if I completely yielded my life to Him. I just had my own idea of what I wanted to do with my life and I was afraid of what giving up my plans for His would mean. I finally let go of my plans to let God have His way in my life, trusting Him whatever that might be. It was a major turning point that took me on a much more significant journey than the one that I had planned myself."

He could either go his own way or trust in God's will. It was time to choose. "You can't have it both ways," he noted. "Ann and I agreed that we would say, 'Whatever You want us to do we will do.' I wasn't sure what God wanted me to do, but 90 percent of the answer is just agreeing to do God's will, whatever it is."

His last year of graduate school, Butch once again taught business calculus. Sharing his faith was easier than ever this time, even though he knew a third of this class were Jewish, raising the odds that there might be backlash. Midway through the semester, Butch delivered his five-minute presentation about his background, explaining, "Christianity has made a huge difference in my life and is the foundation on which everything else is built."

That was at two o'clock. At six thirty that evening Butch got a phone call at home.

"Is this the Bradley who teaches business calculus at UT?" the voice on the line asked.

Uh-oh. The hammer was about to come down on Christianity in the classroom.

"Yes, this is he speaking," Butch answered warily.

"This is Dean Campbell." Campbell was not just a department head or somebody in business school administration; he was dean of students for the entire university.

"I've been through twenty-two Bradleys in the Austin phone book to find you," he said. Walter was the last Bradley on the list. "The Campbell twins in your class are my sons."

Bradley steeled himself for what was coming next. What would the consequences be of him sharing his faith in Jesus? The phone felt clammy in his hand.

"My knees began to shake," he recalled. "But before I had time to have my nervous breakdown, Dean Campbell said, 'I am a Christian. Since my sons have been in college they've wandered off the spiritual reservation, turning their backs on the faith they grew up with. God used whatever you said in your class today to impact them in a really amazing way. They actually walked across campus to my office to tell me what had happened in your class and to discuss their faith.

"'I'm calling to say thank you.'"

What a relief! And what a sign of God's presence. As Butch explained, "If Ann and I ever needed confirmation that being a Christian professor was strategic, I was confirmed by the dean of students at the University of Texas that this was a very, very good thing to do. . . . God could use even the little bit I shared in class in a bigger and more profound way than I ever imagined. God understood that I needed fairly dramatic affirmation. And He gave it to me. . . . I was now very excited to be, for my future students, what no professor had ever been for me: a Christian professor who professed his faith in Jesus Christ."

As he approached the end of his PhD studies in the 1967–68 academic year, Butch began to realize that an academic career gave him the opportunity he wanted to work in math and science and at the same time provided a platform for sharing his faith. And there was a new tool to help him as well. Campus Crusade for Christ began a volunteer associate staff program for college professors called Christian Leadership Ministries, later known as Faculty Commons. By joining, Butch and Ann were privileged to attend CCC staff training with the full-time staff and have some field support from campus staff members at UT or at a nearby university.

When Jim Engel started Christian Leadership Ministry, the faculty ministry of CCC, in 1968, Ann and Walter were his first recruits to be associate staff. "It was this program that ultimately confirmed for Ann and me that my being a Christian professor was God's will for us," Butch later said. "If being a Christian professor was where God wanted me to be, He would take care of my concerns that I might get fired for being even gently identified to my students as a Christian."

Reflecting on his change of heart he observed that originally he "did not want to be a missionary or a minister" but instead had wanted to rise to the top at a technology-driven company. But God's perfect plan combined what Butch wanted with what God wanted. "God's plan was to make me a missionary not to deepest, darkest Africa but to the spiritually deepest and darkest corner of America—secular college campuses—as a Christian professor."

CHAPTER 2

"Everything Happens for a Reason"

Corpus Christi, Texas, was a good place to grow up in the 1950s. A port city of about 150,000 residents on the Gulf of Mexico, it was a community of middle-class families. Many wage earners worked in agriculture, petrochemicals, or the oil and gas industry. Though Corpus Christi was a small city by national standards, its population had tripled in the previous twenty years.

Kenneth and Virginia Bradley moved to Oak Park Avenue, not far from the city center, in 1949 with their two sons, Carl and Walter. It was a Texas homecoming of sorts. Carl had been three years old when Walter was born in Dallas two days after Christmas in 1943. A few years later the Bradleys moved from Dallas to Crowley, Louisiana, where Walter attended first grade in a Catholic school. He loved learning even then. (In the spring he sold the most boxes of candy for a school fundraiser, only to learn that the grand prize was a beautiful rosary—not so interesting for a little Baptist boy.) Now the family was back in Texas to stay. A year after they settled in Oak Park, the Bradleys welcomed a daughter, Linda, to the family.

Kenneth was a civil engineer who directed highway and bridge construction projects. Virginia worked for the Tuloso-Midway School District, first as a teacher and eventually as chief tax assessor and chief financial officer. Walter remembered his father as the biggest spiritual influence in his life during those preteen years and said his mother "was my greatest inspiration to reach for the stars, my greatest cheerleader, and my greatest emotional support, always loving me unconditionally."

Walter went to Oak Park Elementary in the neighborhood, where he was popular and a high achiever. Friends christened him with his nickname, Butch, because his short, blond, flattop haircut looked like a popular cartoon character with that name. One of Butch's favorite activities was reading biographies. The school library had a set of thirty-six of them, bound in orange, that he especially liked. Eventually he read them all. "My mom encouraged me to learn," he said. "She taught me 'don't assume anything is impossible.' She taught me that dreams need a catalyst. You dream out of what you know." He found the lives of these American heroes, many like Lincoln who rose from humble beginnings, were very inspiring.

As a young boy Butch had a knack for working hard and making money. He and his friend Pat Fuggit started a lawn-mowing business together, cutting small lawns with a push mower and hand weeding the flower beds. As Butch later remembered, "It was hard work in the hot Texas sun and only paid fifty cents per lawn, so we chose not to solicit too many customers."

Butch soon found a more attractive alternative. At Oak Park Elementary, students who couldn't afford to buy lunch could earn their meals washing dishes in the cafeteria. That year there were still jobs open after all the qualifying students who wanted the slots had been hired, so the opportunity was opened up to the rest of the school. Butch got permission from his parents to work even though they didn't need the assistance. Butch ate for free, but his mother kept giving him lunch money and let him keep it.

Before long Butch moved on from dishwashing. He got his first paper route when he was eleven years old. Routes were easy to get because nobody wanted to wake up that early to throw papers. His friend Bob Brooks had a route and sometimes Butch helped Bob get his papers ready by rolling them up and tying them with cotton string. Butch thought it looked like a good way to make some money so he applied to the *Corpus Christi Times* to be a paperboy himself and was assigned the route that included his neighborhood. He got up early and threw the morning paper, making the rounds on his bicycle, then made a second daily circuit after school to deliver the afternoon edition.

His friend Bob saved enough to buy a small motorcycle, which meant he could add more accounts and finish his work faster. Again Butch followed in Bob's footsteps, saving his pay and buying a motorcycle of his own. Butch worked for three years without a day off.

In 1955, Butch graduated from elementary school and went on to Driscoll Junior High. Driscoll was fully integrated in response to the recent historic *Brown v. Board of Education* ruling striking down "separate but equal" treatment segregated by race. Butch established easy friendships with Hispanic and African American boys and, as he said, "avoided having the kinds of stereotypes that one has about other races that you know only at a distance." He gathered a large circle of friends and was voted runner-up for Best All Around.

In middle school he continued the violin lessons he'd started in fourth grade and performed in the Driscoll Junior High Orchestra. He enjoyed playing classical music as well as the fiddling hoedown style but would eventually "retire" from playing the violin at the end of the ninth grade.

Though Butch loved sports, he was one of the smaller boys in his class. In Louisiana he'd been allowed to start first grade at the age of five because his birthday was so late in the year, so he was always a year younger than his classmates. This made football and basketball less feasible, but in tennis size wasn't as important. Butch began a lifelong enjoyment of tennis that went on to include a second-place finish in 5A District play as a high school senior and, years later, an intramural division doubles winner at the University of Texas.

Junior high was also when Butch discovered his passion for mathematics. He had endured the boring world of arithmetic for seven long years. Suddenly in the eighth grade everything changed when he discovered the wonders of algebra. Once his algebra teacher allowed him to work ahead, he finished the textbook in about six months and was halfway through the Algebra II text by the end of the year. He finished Algebra II halfway through ninth grade and eagerly went on to geometry. At the end of ninth grade he made the highest grade on the algebra achievement test out of the three hundred students in his class.

At the same time, Butch got to perform his first laboratory experiments, revealing a fascination with science. It was, he later said, "love at first 'bite.'"

The Bradley family were faithful members of the local Baptist church, and Butch regularly invited his schoolmates to church with him. Though he had been baptized when he was eight, there was little change in Butch's life at the time. It was three years later, the summer between elementary school and junior high, that he believed God had touched his heart in a special way. More than sixty years later he still remembers the date vividly. On June 6, 1955, during a weeklong camp with his church youth group, Butch Bradley made a life-changing profession of faith. For the first time ever, Jesus became real to him, and he began to experience remarkable changes.

Butch was so excited by this newfound relationship that he started reading five chapters of the Bible every day, tenaciously working his way through the lofty King James translation with its unfamiliar words and sentence structure. Recalling the experience he said, "Because of my newly found and passionate desire to know Jesus better, I longed for the 'pure milk of the Word' that the apostle Peter described in my King James text: 'Wherefore laying aside all malice, and all guile, and hypocrisies, and envies, and all evil speakings, as newborn babes, desire the sincere milk of the word, that ye may grow thereby'" (1 Peter 2:1–2).

Butch read the first nineteen books of the Bible, Genesis through Psalms, before his zeal to comprehend the King James version was finally exhausted. Though he stopped his daily reading, he continued diligently to love God and to do his best to lead a moral life. Yet it would be years before he understood that the Holy Spirit was the only agent of change that could make him into the person God wanted him to be. As Paul described it, "The fruit of the Spirit is love, joy, peace, patience, kindness, goodness, faith, gentleness, self-control; against such things there is no law" (Galatians 5:22–23). A more complete transformation would come during college after meeting like-minded people in Campus Crusade for Christ who could provide the additional teaching and fellowship Butch needed.

Meanwhile, Butch continued attending middle school, delivering newspapers, playing tennis, and exploring the world of algebra and geometry. He and his friends entertained themselves doing what most boys in the neighborhood did: they built forts out of cardboard boxes, ran their bicycles through mud puddles, designed and made box kites, and played sandlot games and Little League baseball together. His buddies marveled at Butch's model airplane collection on display in his bedroom. The world these boys lived in invoked the confident idealism of Norman Rockwell's mid-century America.

It was an idyllic way of life that ended too soon in a burst of tragic violence.

On Monday, August 4, 1958, Butch, age fourteen, was on a weeklong camping trip with his friend Bob Brooks and the Brooks family at Garner State Park near Concan, Texas. It was near the same place that Butch had met Jesus in such a profound way three summers before. A highway patrol officer came to their campsite and said there was a family emergency in the Bradley household and that Butch needed to get home immediately. The Brookses took Butch to the nearby town of Uvalde and put him on a Greyhound bus back to Corpus Christi. He made the trip anxiously wondering what kind of emergency was waiting for him at home.

Stepping off the bus in Corpus Christi, Butch was met by his family pastor, Reverend Kenneth Hiner. Upon seeing him, Butch knew something terrible must have happened. It was the pastor's sad duty to tell the teenager about an event that from then on would be the biggest tragedy and puzzle of Butch Bradley's life: for no apparent reason, his father had shot and killed Butch's eighteen-year-old brother, Carl, in the bedroom the two brothers shared and then had taken his own life. His mother had been asleep in a front bedroom next to seven-year-old Linda's bedroom. She heard Walter's father get up about five thirty that morning and thought he was going for a drink of water. Virginia heard a muffled pop, followed by a second pop. Leaving her sleeping daughter, she hurried to the back bedroom and found her husband and son dead on the floor. Each had a single gunshot wound to the head. Kenneth's .22 rifle was under his body. Horrified and in shock, Virginia took her daughter to a neighbor's house and called the police. Kenneth Bradley was forty-six.

"Everything changed that day," Butch stated when recounting those dark moments. "I became the man in my home overnight out of necessity.

I made a promise to God and my mom that I would never act like a stupid teenager and would help her in every way I could. I also promised Linda that I would try to be a surrogate father to her."

The Bradley family tragedy was front-page news in Corpus Christi. As a self-proclaimed "typical socially insecure sophomore," Butch dreaded going back to school and facing all the questions and inquiring looks. To his surprise and relief, classmates and neighbors were kind enough not to ask him about it even once.

He knew he needed to figure out how to accept what had happened and move on with life. He held on to the good memories of his father. "My father was a great dad," Butch said. "His work kept him on the road most of the week, but when he was home we had lots of fun together. One of our favorite family treats was when Dad took us to the drive-in movies. He made a picnic meal for us to eat in the car while we watched the show." Now all that was gone.

"My father was a very committed Christian," Butch continued. "He and Mom used to argue about whether to give their 10 percent tithe at the beginning of the month or at the end. Mom said they should give it at the end if they had enough money left. Dad believed they should give it at the beginning and trust God to get them through the rest of the month.

"Sometimes our church had a twenty-four-hour prayer chain in advance of some special event. My father would always sign up for the 2:00–3:00 a.m. hour and would invite me to come pray with him. He demonstrated his love of God and his family in so many ways. How could such a devout Christian kill his son and then take his own life? I knew that someday I would see clearly how God used this in my life."

It was twenty years before Butch understood, at least in part, how such a tragedy could happen and how God could use it for good. As he explained, "When my sister was in her mid-twenties, she was diagnosed as being manic depressive bipolar, a syndrome that was not yet fully recognized in 1958. I also had a close friend later in my life, an outstanding professor at Texas A&M University, who struggled with being manic depressive bipolar and eventually committed suicide, leaving a wife and three children. Through him I was able to see the kind of struggles my father must have had. I'm sure now that my father was bipolar, but we had no understanding of that kind of problem in 1958.

"Subsequently my sister's son, Brad, was also diagnosed with manic depression. Fortunately for them both, medical science had advanced by then and developed treatment options that were pretty effective. Along with following the medical advances, I carefully studied the book of Job, the oldest book in the Bible. The lessons there were of great comfort and helped me understand that God will not necessarily reveal the 'why' to me. But He does promise that He will walk with me through the journey, giving me sufficient strength to carry on. And He has kept that promise faithfully."

Finally, Butch "came to understand why my father might have taken my brother with him to heaven. Carl was dyslexic, before we understood how to diagnose or treat it. His difficulty in seeing letters correctly meant that he had difficulty reading, causing him to fall behind as he got to higher grades that required more reading to succeed. I think my father was worried about how Carl would manage if he could not graduate from high school, which was a possibility.

"Everything happens for a reason," Walter observed, looking back on those events through years of life experience. "God doesn't cause bad things to happen, but He does use them for good."

The shock of his father's death, and the memory of it more than half a century later, underscore the power of faith in Walter's life when all other powers fall short. "Look again at Paul's writing," he suggested. In Paul's letter to the Romans he wrote, "We also rejoice in our afflictions, because we know that affliction produces endurance, endurance produces proven character, and proven character produces hope. This hope does not disappoint us, because God's love has been poured out in our hearts through the Holy Spirit who was given to us" (Romans 5:3–5 csb). Later in his letter Paul underscored his point with a powerful affirmation, declaring, "We know that all things work together for the good of those who love God: those who are called according to His purpose" (Romans 8:28).

Virginia Bradley was bitter for ten years after her husband's murder-suicide. It would have been perfectly understandable for Butch to become bitter as well—either angry with God or convinced there was no God. Butch's newly found Christian faith and relationship with Jesus literally saved his life, though he easily could have become an atheist. By God's grace, the experience strengthened him and made him determined to be a better son to his mother and a better brother to Linda. He even earned a hardship driver's license at fourteen so he could help his mother with errands and take his sister to and from school.

Butch's mother was a CPA when her husband died. As a single mother of two, she took a job as tax assessor and collector and financial manager for the Tuloso Midway School District. Walter kept his paper route for another year as life gradually returned to normal. He stayed in the Boy Scouts, earned the God and Country award, and worked his way up to Eagle rank.

In 1958, Butch graduated from Driscoll Junior High and that fall started the tenth grade at Roy Miller High School. Determined to keep earning his own spending money, he got a job after school cleaning cars on a used car lot. When he was fifteen, the summer after his sophomore year in high school, he found a job as a construction worker installing air-conditioning units at the new Corpus Christi airport terminal. He worked for the same contractor after his junior and senior years as well. He learned what he called the "silly rules" of labor unions that prohibited him doing anything that involved tools on the job, even simple tasks, as a way of creating more union jobs and significantly increasing the cost of construction.

In high school, Butch developed into an excellent tennis player, lettering all three years at Miller High and winning second place in his 5A district his senior year. He was also elected one of two male cheerleaders (male cheerleaders were common in the South even in the 1950s) and was a fixture at football games and other athletic events. The routines were simple by today's standards, though Butch liked to do flips at pep rallies and football games. Friends remember him occasionally hitting the top of his head and coming out of the move rubbing his flattop.

The Miller High Buccaneers played a great season in 1960, eventually winning the Texas state football championship that year, with Butch and his fellow cheerleaders whipping up the fans every week. Unlike much of the South in those days, the Buccaneers were a racially integrated team with nineteen white, six black, and eighteen Hispanic players. Their championship year, the star quarterback and the coach were both Hispanic and the top running back was black. This posed a challenge when the team traveled out of town to cities where black players weren't allowed to stay in local motels. The team refused to stay where everyone was not welcomed and would drive to the next town to find a motel that would accept all the players.

As the end of his high school career approached, Butch was excited to go to college, a dream his mother had fostered in him from an early age. Both of his parents had graduated from college at a time when only 20 percent of Americans had college degrees.

Friends during those years remember his unfailing kindness and his "special grin." They saw him as a Christian gentleman—"though not a goodie two-shoes"—who never said a bad thing about anybody; and nobody ever said anything bad about him. Years later one of his cheerleading partners remembered him as "one of the sweetest, kindest, smartest young men I knew." He was known for enthusiastically participating in neighborhood dances hosted in his friends' garages, where they scattered cornmeal on the floor to dance. Friends recall Butch was "always teaching people, keeping them out of trouble, and encouraging them by word and example to explore a relationship with Jesus."

During his high school career Butch kept up his faithful church attendance, regularly inviting his friends to come along. He promised them that not only was the Baptist church interesting and fun, there were more girls there than at the Methodist church. He went steady with Mary Myers for two of his high school years. He sometimes took his little sister, Linda, along on dates. In the absence of a father figure, including her was one way he felt he could be the better brother he had promised to be.

Butch graduated third in his class of 615 from Roy Miller High in the spring of 1961. Then, at the age of seventeen, he headed north to Austin to start his college career at the University of Texas. Because he received an honorable mention (Letter of Commendation) on the National Merit Scholarship exam (top 2 percent), Butch was invited to be in the UT honors program in engineering science, a special preparation for students who demonstrated outstanding potential and who knew they wanted to go to graduate school. The classes were limited to fifteen to twenty students and taught by the best professor in the department for each topic. As a result, Butch received the equivalent of an Ivy League education for in-state tuition of fifty dollars per semester.

Low though his college tuition was, Butch still had to come up with money for his books, fees, and living expenses. There was almost no financial aid for undergraduates. His first year he worked as a paper grader, moving gradually up the ranks in later years to lecture assistant (supervising other paper graders) and teaching labs.

For three years in high school, Butch had worked summers in construction. The summer after his first year at Texas, he landed a job that paid 30 percent more. He jumped at the chance for a substantial raise, even though the work was a hundred percent more unpleasant. His new job was to unload boxcars full of grain at the Port of Corpus Christi. Some of the grain fell out the side doors of the cars when the doors were opened. The rest of it had to be shoveled by hand onto an auger that carried it out of the car. Butch took the night shift, climbing into cars and shoveling from midnight until eight a.m. unless it rained. It was hot, dusty, backbreaking work. He had to wear goggles, long sleeves, gloves, a neck cover, and a respirator to avoid inhaling the grain dust. That summer of 1962 there was a long drought in Corpus Christi. As a result, he worked eighty-nine nights in a row without a night off.

Butch embraced the challenge with typical resolve. He earned 150 percent of his regular wages for overtime on the sixth and seventh work night of every week. That made him grateful for the drought and the long stretch of time on the job. He would need every penny for college the coming term. "An important part of what God has done in my life is to give me an appreciation for the value of work and empathy for people who do manual labor their whole lives," he said. "The capacity to enjoy work and not resent it is a real blessing."

One of the first realities that hit Butch at the University of Texas was that college was a lot harder than high school. Accustomed to making top grades, Butch ended his freshman year with a 3.6 GPA, which was still sufficient to be inducted into Pi Tau Sigma, the freshman honor society. But like many college students, Butch procrastinated during much of the term, then crammed frantically for exams. The next year his study habits improved dramatically, though the inspiration was nothing he could have imagined. During his sophomore year at UT, Butch learned for a second time in his life that God can cause all things to work together for those who love Him and are called according to His purposes, even if in the short term some of those things seem like absolute disasters.

It was February 1963. Butch had joined the Sigma Nu fraternity and liked hanging around with his fellow fraternity brothers. One afternoon he was running across the back patio toward the fraternity house. As a prank, one of his fraternity brothers dropped a plastic laundry bag full of water from the second floor. It exploded on the patio in front of a large sliding glass door, soaking the area Butch was running toward and instantly rendering the surface as slick as ice. The glass door was open. Unfortunately, as Butch made a sharp turn and slipped, he missed the opening and sailed feetfirst through both the stationary four-by-eight-foot panel of glass beside the sliding door and the sliding door itself, which when open was positioned behind the stationary panel. Butch landed on his back, half in and half out of the room. His legs and feet broke out the bottom halves of both panels of glass. An instant later, the top halves came sliding down like a guillotine, stripping the skin off his shins, puncturing his chest between the stomach and lungs, and missing vital organs by inches. He was rushed to the hospital, where it took a surgeon four hours to close his nineteen major wounds with 319 stitches.

Butch spent a week recovering in the student health center. Though he had excused absences for the classes he missed, he still had to take upcoming exams for the first five weeks in six subjects on the regular schedule because his professors didn't want to write and grade makeup tests. On his first round of exams he made one C and five Ds.

Instead of admitting defeat, Butch radically altered his study habits and dramatically changed his approach to learning. He started carefully planning his time to be sure he was studying twenty-five hours or more each week. He read his textbook sections before the professor presented them in class, which greatly increased his in-class learning. That in turn significantly reduced the time it took to solve his homework problems. He studied as if he had exams every Friday.

When exam time came around again, Butch was thoroughly prepared, felt relatively stress-free, and didn't have to cram at the last minute. "Struggling to catch up after my accident helped me become the good student I became and develop the study habits that were the foundation of my subsequent academic success," he later observed. "It wasn't God's predestination for me to run through a glass window. But He did use it to make me a great student. I also realized I didn't have to choose between doing my academic work and having fun."

Butch had a far better experience during the next round of exams. By then he had brought his C and five Ds up to four Bs and two Cs—still not very good, he thought. But thanks to his new study regimen, without studying at all for finals (he went to four movies instead) he aced every one of them and raised his final grades to five As and a B. It would be the best semester results of his four years as an undergraduate. "If you keep up with things you'll never have to worry about them," he realized. "Procrastination is giving up on your dreams one day at a time."

By the end of the spring semester Butch had recovered completely. His summer job that year was one of his most strenuous ever: working as a roustabout and roughneck on an oil rig in Houma, Louisiana, southwest of New Orleans in the Mississippi River delta. This was hard, dirty, dangerous work, twelve hours on and twelve hours off, seven days a week. But it paid well and allowed him to return to school with a substantial sum in the bank for a change.

The spring of his junior year Butch was invited to join the Silver Spurs honorary society. New members, who were invited by standing members, were limited to around ten students per semester out of a campus enrollment of thirty thousand. Selection was based on demonstrated leadership and service on the University of Texas campus and outstanding achievements. One of the society's highest profile honors was taking care of the school mascot, a live Texas longhorn named Bevo, during football games. Another honor was acting as driver for dignitaries who visited the UT campus or who came to the state capitol. "Silver Spurs provided many rich opportunities to serve," Butch later wrote. "What a wonderful experience for a young college student."

Also in the spring of 1964, Butch was inducted into Tau Beta Phi, the national honors engineering fraternity. He went to the initiation banquet

Walter Bradley, kneeling lower right, as a member of UT Austin's Silver Spurs honorary society charged with care of mascot longhorn steer, Bevo, during football games.

on a double date with his friend and fellow engineering student Eddie Miller. Eddie's date that night was a co-ed from Dallas named Carol Ann Jones, known to her friends as Ann. That fall, as Butch started his senior year, the Silver Spurs planned a big social event in Dallas for the second weekend in October to attend the football game against Oklahoma, which was one of their biggest rivals. For such a special event, every student wanted an equally special date. Since Butch couldn't afford a hotel room for his date, his plan was to find a date whose family lived in Dallas. Ann was the perfect solution.

To test the waters, Butch invited Ann out on what he called "a Coke date." He had a great time and at the end of the evening asked Ann if she would like to go to the OU-Texas football game and the Silver Spurs party in Dallas. Not only did she say yes, she offered him a place to stay. Her parents were hosting a houseful of sorority sisters, and her mother said Butch would be welcome too if he didn't mind sleeping in the dining room. He accepted the family hospitality, and he and Ann enjoyed their

Ann and Walter renewed their marriage vows on their fiftieth wedding anniversary in 2015. And then they danced.

big weekend together. God had again used the "blessing" of poverty to direct him to Ann, "my wonder mate for life." Soon they were inseparable.

Butch invited Ann along when the Silver Spurs gave him the honor of driving Governor Pat Brown of California and his wife from Austin to the LBJ Ranch, home of President Lyndon Johnson, for a barbecue celebrating Johnson's recent election as president. They made the trip in a sharp-looking Cadillac convertible provided by a local dealer. The more Butch and Ann saw of each other, the more they wanted to see.

The two got engaged the following March and married at the end of August 1965 after Butch finished his undergraduate studies. Butch recalled, "We really couldn't afford to get married, but that summer I got a telegram from the National Science Foundation saying I'd been selected to receive a prestigious National Science Foundation Fellowship to pay my tuition, fees, books, and living expenses for three years. It also had a modest $50-a-month dependent allowance." The pay was $250 a month, with an extra $50 per month for married students. The situation would call for living on a very lean budget, and Ann had one more year of college to go. "She agreed to live in poverty for one year, then get a teaching job after she graduated," Butch said.

In 1965, Butch received his bachelor's degree in engineering science. True to form, he rolled right into his graduate studies in materials science.

It wasn't long before he started teaching math classes and sharing his Christian identity with the freshman business school classes. And it also wasn't long before Butch was reminded once more of how fleeting and delicate life can be.

The summer after his first year of graduate school, Butch was taking classes and helping out at the ME office on campus. Monday, August 1, 1966, was a typical Texas summer day. By late morning the temperature was nearly a hundred degrees, the clear sky bleached almost white by the unrelenting sun. Pavement radiated the heat back into the air, trapping pedestrians between the layers like a convection oven.

Every day between his late-morning class and lunch, Butch walked across campus to pick up the ME department mail at the university post office. Usually he headed out about 11:45 a.m. This particular Monday he was running late (for all his limitless energy, Butch had already acquired a reputation for running late) and decided to go after his next class instead.

The change in routine probably saved his life. "If I had been where I almost always was," he said, "I would have been one of the first dead."

At 11:48 that morning, an architectural engineering student named Charles Whitman started shooting at random from the twenty-eighth-floor observation deck of the landmark clock tower in the center of campus. He fired his rifle at everything that moved. Had Butch been on his regular schedule, he would have been walking on the mall at the foot of the tower when the gunman opened fire.

Whitman, twenty-five, was an ex-Marine sharpshooter who served in Cuba and had been discharged the year before. He killed seventeen people in all before police took him down, including his mother and wife, whom he had shot earlier, an unborn child whose mother was hit, and a victim who died in 2001. Thirty-one were wounded, the worst of whom was blinded and paralyzed.

Butch had had a brush with tragedy when his father and brother died. Years later he miraculously survived running through a sliding glass door. Now he was saved from almost certain death at the hands of a deranged killer. Butch was convinced that God's protective hand had once again saved him for a greater purpose.

But what was that greater purpose? Now that Butch had dedicated himself to serving Christ, what form would that service take?

One possibility was in the exciting, rapidly expanding field of space exploration. The first US astronaut had ventured into space only five years earlier. In 1963, John Glenn became the first American to orbit the earth. NASA's spacecraft development program generated tremendous interest in the field of materials science where components of rockets that would carry men to the moon and supersonic airliners that would race westward, beating the sun across the sky and delivering passengers to New York before the time their watches showed them leaving Paris or London, were being invented.

Companies in every field of science and industry were expanding and increasing their budgets for research and development. Butch set his sights on landing a job and building a career with one of them. But as he started his final year of school in the fall of 1967, he found himself rethinking his plan to get a job in industry. It wasn't for a lack of opportunity. He had offers to interview with eighteen sterling multinational corporations. He traveled to ten interviews, getting four job offers from the first five, including DuPont and General Electric, before canceling the rest. Ann would soon deliver their first child, and he was nervous about being away. The jobs would have all been in the Northeast, and Butch and Ann didn't want to live in that part of the country. And as his student years came to an end, Butch Bradley felt the pull of a challenge taking him in a direction he had never imagined.

To Butch, American college campuses had become a spiritual wasteland. So many great centers of learning started out with strong ties to Christianity. Now many of them rejected faith, some of them vehemently. Colleges were deep, dark places where Christianity was mocked, ignored, hidden, practiced almost in secret. No one wanted to be branded an anti-intellectual dullard with no more sense than to believe those crazy stories in the Bible.

Yet Butch didn't want future students to have the same college experience he did, not knowing a single Christian teacher on campus. He determined he could be an example to them. He would not bend to the pressure to conform. Nor would he wear his faith on his sleeve or use it as an excuse for anything less than excellent performance. If he was going to identify himself as a Christian to the academic world, he was going to be the best. He wouldn't preach or evangelize, but he wouldn't hide his faith under a bushel basket either.

He realized this approach could get him in hot water with his colleagues, his administration, and his students, but he didn't care. He would hold fast to his principles. "With eighteen interview offers I knew I could always go into industry later," he recalled. "I decided I would try being a Christian professor. If I get fired I'll do something else. I went into teaching not to be a college professor alone, but to have an influence; to be a Christian professor."

The summer Butch got his PhD, he and Ann went to Arrowhead Springs near San Bernardino, California, for training with the Christian Leadership Ministry of Campus Crusade for Christ. Campus Crusade had recently purchased the classic Arrowhead Springs Hotel as its headquarters. When Butch and Ann arrived, the first thing they learned was that they weren't actually supposed to be there. "You can't just show up," Butch was told. "You have to apply, have references, submit an application, be interviewed, etc. Somehow we didn't know that." But they were welcomed nonetheless and soon were immersed in training to lead campus ministry. The program gave them general information on how to support the on-campus efforts and appeal to students.

It helped confirm Butch's decision to pursue an academic career, and he made one more decision as he redirected his focus from a corporate research scientist to the classroom. He went back to calling himself Walter. After all, whoever heard of a college professor named Butch?

CHAPTER 3

Breaking Through Barriers

Once Walter Bradley decided to become a college professor instead of a corporate executive, he had to refocus his job search in a hurry. It was January 1968, very late in the academic hiring cycle, before he started looking for a tenure-track engineering position to begin that fall. By then his competition had been submitting applications for months. Colleges looking for new professors were well into the process of recruiting and interviewing. Typically the department with the opening had a committee to go through résumés, schedule phone interviews, and then about Christmas or January invite the finalists to campus.

Against long odds, Walter began applying for fall 1968 openings and visited three schools that had positions available. He also asked his department head, Professor Bill Upthegrove, if he knew of any possibilities. Dr. Upthegrove called a friend of his, Dr. Al Schlechten, head of the Department of Metallurgical Engineering at the Colorado School of Mines (CSM), which had the second-ranked program in the United States. Dr. Schlechten said, "I didn't have an opening until this morning. I had an argument with a professor in my department and he resigned on the spot. It's too late to do a national search for a replacement so we're scrambling to fill the position." Immediately Dr. Upthegrove recommended Walter in glowing terms. "Send me his résumé," Dr. Schlechten said, "and we will consider him." It was, Bradley thought, the first clear indication that he was headed in the right direction with his career decision.

Usually positions like this were filled only after a nationwide search. Dr. Schlechten called Walter the following Monday after he had reviewed Walter's outstanding credentials and invited him to come for an interview Friday of the same week, then offered him a tenure track assistant professorship before he left campus. Walter would teach Introduction to Physical Metallurgy, a junior year class, and an Introduction to Solid State Physics for graduate students.

Walter's first teaching experience—and his first experience sharing his faith in class—at the University of Texas had been a low-risk opportunity. At worst, he would have lost his graduate teaching job, which paid peanuts (though welcome peanuts they were). Now he was a tenure-track professor with a real career on the line, plus a new baby and a pregnant wife to support. Yet the way the whole process at CSM had unfolded made Walter and Ann feel they were in the center of God's will, reminding them of the promise in Proverbs 3:5–6: "Trust in the LORD with all your heart, and do not rely on your own understanding; in all your ways know him, and he will make your paths straight." Besides, as Walter told himself, if it didn't work out—if he couldn't teach and be open about his faith—he could always take a corporate job like one of the many he'd been offered.

Though Walter had been a Christian for some time by now, by his own admission he was not all that mature. He and Ann were two well-meaning people "who had good hearts but didn't really know what we were doing." The whole adventure would be a growing process for them both.

As the verse in Proverbs directed, Walter trusted that he would find ways to share his faith with the academic community. "We always felt that God was guiding and directing us," he said, "because we got too many things right. Looking back, I can say, 'Wow, that was really pretty impactful.' But I also have to be humble and say, 'No it wasn't us; it was God pointing us this way and pushing us that way.'" The couple's time in Colorado turned out to be eight of the most amazing years of their lives.

As he considered the opportunities ahead, Walter saw unmistakable parallels between modern-day Christians in academia and the children of Israel. God promised to take His chosen people to the promised land flowing with milk and honey—a land of great opportunity but also great risks. He led Walter and Ann to Colorado and an environment full of both risks and potential rewards. In that situation, Walter hoped he would be like Caleb and Joshua in the Bible, who encouraged other Israelites to trust God in challenging times and trusted that He would carry them through safely.

Walter also saw his and Ann's experience reflected in John Bunyan's *Pilgrim's Progress*, where Christian goes on a journey in search of God's will for his life. Walter's objective was to be a Christian professor who demonstrated both by action and word that he was a follower of Jesus who withstood the pressure to hide his light under a bushel. Looking back later Walter observed, "Becoming a Christian professor was much more challenging than I realized when I began this quest and so much more rewarding than I could have dreamed. It was a step that challenged and forever changed our lives."

Letting his light shine would mean going against the status quo at Colorado School of Mines. And he wasn't going to get a lot of help from his colleagues. A recently retired CSM professor who attended the church Walter and Ann joined told them that he knew of only one other Christian professor on campus and said less than 5 percent of the students had any church background.

Walter had to reach out in a way no one on campus was doing. He felt like the shoe salesman who arrived in Africa in 1920 and realized that no one wore shoes. His boss responded, "This is terrific! Everyone is a prospective customer." Walter said, "If Christians form a circle on the lawn after church on Sunday, strike matches, and sing, 'This little light of mine, I'm going to let it shine,' it will have little, if any, impact. If Christians choose to go to spiritually dark places like public universities to strike their matches, it could make a huge difference."

Walter wanted to be the exception to the rule at CSM, living out and sharing his faith regardless of what others did, though he couldn't help feeling apprehensive. Yet he wanted not to worry about what other people thought; he wanted to please God first. The young professor looked for guidance in the story of the apostle Paul, who was stoned for preaching the gospel. The apostle Paul considered it a small thing that he should be judged by any human court; ultimately he was concerned only about whether Christ was honored. He wanted to live his life in a way that would be pleasing to Him first. Paul was playing to an audience of one regardless of the consequences. That's what Walter wanted to do in his own life. His first university position was the perfect place to start.

Settling into their new surroundings, the Bradleys sensed that their faculty colleagues were both sort of appalled by and sort of curious about their Christianity. But they never felt mistreatment or hostility from Walter's colleagues or their spouses, though they did experience indifference. "The real openness," Walter recalled, "was with students." He reasoned you go through the door that God opens and don't try to beat on the one that's closed. The Bradleys started the first Christian student group in the history of Colorado School of Mines, then had the wonderful experience of seeing God bless it in ways far beyond what they could have imagined.

During Dr. Bradley's first semester at CSM, he decided hanging a poster in his office was one way to identify himself as a follower of Jesus— a friendly, nonconfrontational approach that nonetheless made a clear statement. In a local Christian bookstore he and Ann bought a poster with a big, colorful peace symbol and the pithy message, "If you want real peace, follow Jesus!" The two of them prayed on a Monday morning at breakfast about this first step in Walter's journey to becoming a professing "Christian professor."

But in a repeat of what happened at the University of Texas, he put the poster on his office bulletin board, then soon took it down, "overcome with my fear of what my colleagues might think if they came into my office." That night Ann asked if he got any comments on the poster. Walter could tell she was disappointed when he admitted he'd taken it down. "I also wished that I had gotten a poster that was more innocuous and prudent," he later wrote, "maybe a beautiful waterfall with an obscure quotation about living water," something Christians would understand but that would be unrecognizable to secular students and colleagues.

Tuesday was a repeat of the day before: the poster went up, the poster went down, with Walter sheepishly admitting to Ann he had once again lost his nerve. Wednesday he promised God that the poster would go up and stay up as long as he was at CSM. It wasn't long before his resolve was put to the test. A Unitarian colleague dropped by mid-morning and couldn't help but notice the large, colorful poster in the room. But after glancing at it, the professor started talking about business he came to transact without any mention of the poster. "In time, most of my students and all of my colleagues saw it," Walter said. "Some commented on it, but most did not. While it did not start many conversations, it clearly identified me as a follower of Jesus and sowed seeds in the hearts of my guests during the eight years I was at CSM."

As a graduate student teaching in Texas, Walter had explained to students that he identified himself as a Christian not to impose his faith on them but to help them understand who he was and why he treated them with respect and kindness. One day midway through his first semester at CSM, he felt the time was right to do the same with his new classes. "I briefly shared some personal details about myself to help my approximately one hundred students get to know me better as a person, not just as their teacher," he said. He also passed out three-by-five cards and asked them to write down interesting facts about themselves so that he could know them as a person and not just as a student.

His explanation to the class went something like this: "I have a wonderful wife, Ann, whom I met my senior year in college and married the summer after I got my BS degree. We have a daughter who was born the spring of my last year in graduate school and a son who will be born this coming spring. I love to play tennis, which I played competitively in high school, and racquetball, which I recently started. I love to snow ski and am an avid jogger. Ann is a gypsy who loves to travel and so do I. Our bucket list includes visiting all seven continents some day and living on at least three before we expire. But the most important thing you should know about me is that I became a follower of Jesus Christ as a college student after pursuing success as my god and finding that success alone did not really satisfy. I hope you will see it makes a great deal of difference in how I treat you in this class. I would be glad to visit outside of class with anyone who would like to know more about my faith journey."

That night Walter got a call from the editor of the campus newspaper, the *Oredigger*. Three different students had contacted him to report some unusual but interesting things their professor of Introduction to Physical Metallurgy had shared in class and encouraged him to invite Dr. Bradley to write a guest article on the topic. "Sometimes God-ordained opportunity comes not as a door, but as a dare," Bradley observed.

Because the *Oredigger* published only once a week and included all the relevant campus news, it was widely read by the student body. To Walter it was a wonderful opportunity to share his testimony with the whole school at once. That excitement was partly offset by knowing his secular colleagues would also read his article and see his picture. What would they think? Could this prejudice his tenure review? Maybe even get him fired?

Thinking the offer through, Walter reflected on the Bible passage from the gospel of John, substituting the words of his own situation for the one described in Scripture: "Many did believe in him even among the rulers [professors], but because of the Pharisees [deans and department heads] they did not confess him, so that they would not be banned from the synagogue [university]. For they loved human praise more than praise from God" (12:42–43).

With that in mind, Walter felt at peace about writing the article. He saw it as the latest in a series of barriers to sharing his faith that he had broken through. The first breakthrough was finally sharing his Christian testimony with his students at the University of Texas after dozens of false starts. The second was putting up a Christian poster in his office at CSM; that time it took only three tries. The third and boldest breakthrough was the campus newspaper article, which he enthusiastically completed on the first try to encouraging results. Quite a few students mentioned it to him afterward, though not one colleague ever did.

Walter prayed that God would give him the daily grace to honor his commitment to his students and that they would see a difference in the way he treated them. He took his students' pictures in small groups the first day of class and used the photos to learn their names quickly. He took time to visit personally with them when they came by for homework help. Soon he was going snow skiing and playing tennis with some of them at their invitation.

Faith and friendship, however, did not dilute academic standards. Engineering is a tough discipline, and Dr. Bradley didn't soften the blow.

He wanted to make sure his students approached the field with their eyes wide open. Better that they should be sure of their commitment and realize the challenges up front rather than later when it would be harder to change majors. Dr. Bradley set ambitious learning objectives, then worked hard to help every student master them with well-crafted lectures and homework assignments. He held optional yet well-attended review sessions the night before his exams that began at 7 p.m. and went until the students ran out of questions.

Professor Bradley was twenty-four when he started his career at CSM. His younger students were around twenty, and the graduate students in his classes were the same age he was. This made it easy to connect both socially and spiritually with them. Walter considered it providential that presidents of four fraternities and the student body president were in his first class at the school. This yielded opportunities for him to talk about his faith at several fraternity houses during the spring semester. Enough members were drawn to Christianity that he started Bible studies for new believers at SAE and Sigma Nu. Students also came to Sunday-night Bible studies in the Bradleys' home with, as Walter described it, "the bait being a delicious dinner prepared by Ann each week, an amazing feat for a mother of a ten-month-old who was pregnant with her second baby." Students in this first Bible study became the foundation for the Christian ministry at CSM.

Walter and Ann also wanted to reach out to their faculty colleagues and to their neighbors in the new faculty apartment housing. They saw an opportunity in the testimony Ann heard at a Christian Women's Club in Denver of a woman from India who became a Christian from a high Hindu sect while at Harvard. The Bradleys invited all the professors and spouses in Walter's department, his department head, dean, and provost, along with his and Ann's faculty apartment neighbors to hear the woman share her story. While an evening like that in Texas would not be too unusual, it was a novelty in secular Colorado where only about 5 percent of residents went to church.

Ann and Walter invited eighteen couples because they figured that only one-third at most would come. Remarkably, all eighteen arrived. They spilled off the living room furniture onto the floor, sat in the dining room, stood in the kitchen, and squeezed in wherever they could. Clearly the invitation had piqued their interest. Ann and Walter were thrilled to have so many friends and colleagues join them to hear this woman's wonderful experience.

Walter's office poster and his feature in the *Oredigger* had sowed some seeds with his colleagues after all. The former Hindu gave a powerful and inspiring presentation. After she finished, one of Walter's colleagues asked if she believed everyone in the room who didn't believe in Jesus was going to hell. As she was taking a moment to formulate her answer, her tactless husband jumped in, aggressively confronting the questioner, and the discussion quickly degenerated into a heated and hopelessly unproductive forty-five-minute turn-or-burn session. It was a disastrous Pandora's box that was impossible to close.

"Ann and I were horrified!" Walter later wrote. "When the rancorous discussion finally ran its course, we quickly served dessert and everyone went home. Had we been able to access a U-Haul truck that evening, we would have almost surely loaded it and left for Texas. Lord, why did such a promising evening go up in smoke?" He could imagine the administration deciding this was one new tenure-track professor they definitely didn't want in their department.

He went to bed thinking, "My peachy career is coming to an early end!" The next morning he woke up to the grim reality of going to campus and facing his colleagues. "It was the most difficult day of my entire career," he recalled. He wrote that he considered calling in "(heart)sick," but knew he wouldn't be well any time soon. There was no point in delaying the inevitable.

To his amazement, his colleagues were extremely gracious, saying such things as, "That was a really interesting evening at your apartment last night. I've never been to anything like it before." Walter felt like saying, "Neither have I!"

"I learned two important lessons through this very painful experience," Walter said of that unforgettable night. "First, God can work through even our greatest failed programs to advance His kingdom. No matter how big my blunders, God can get my fat out of the fire.

"Second, once your reputation is as ruined as it could possibly be, you will have real freedom from the worry of what people will think. After this debacle (humanly speaking), Ann and I were free to do whatever we felt God was leading us to do, knowing that we could not possibly have a worse event than the one we'd just had, and that God had supernaturally superintended it to His (and our) benefit. God gave us favor beyond anything I could expect."

Far from being defeated by their experience, Walter and Ann used it to start the ball rolling for regular events in their home. They set aside one night per month to invite various non-Christian couples over for dinner. Ann was also invited to speak to the Mines Wives Club at CSM. Ann shared her faith journey of coming from a non-Christian home and finding Christ as a sophomore in college reading the Bible by herself. Seven of the wives at the presentation asked Ann if she could lead a Bible study for them, which she gladly agreed to do. One by one, all came to faith in Jesus. They then requested a couples Bible study in the hope that their husbands might join them in their newfound faith. Ann and Walter hosted this study in their home as Ann had done with the ladies. In time all the husbands followed their wives to faith in Christ, and the couples study continued as long as the husbands were students at Mines.

As this couples study came to end due to the graduation of the married students, Walter started a new couples study with Ann in their home for international students. The group was initially mixed with some Christians and some seekers. Eventually all became Christians and several remained lifelong friends. Carlos and Dirce Coutinho later made it possible for the whole Bradley family to have an unforgettable adventure in Brazil. Dr. and Mrs. Soo Woo Nam from South Korea became lifelong friends, and over time arranged several visits to South Korea for Dr. Bradley to speak both professionally on materials science and engineering and in churches and at national conferences for Christian professors on faith and science.

Walter continued leading Bible studies throughout the school year while also building interest in the Campus Crusade for Christ ministry that was developing. Inspired at least in part by Dr. Bradley, the student body president persuaded the student senate to sponsor a fundraising concert that spring by the New Folk, a Christian singing group with CCC. The group had a couple of LP albums to their credit and was on a nationwide tour of college campuses that year.

The show at CSM was a sellout, with over 500 students attending out of a campus of 1,600. The New Folk were one of the many groups capitalizing on the folk music craze. There were nine singers in matching outfits, the men with short, trim haircuts and the women with blonde bouffants. Two men also played guitars, with another on banjo and one on upright bass. They interspersed traditional folk songs with current pop selections like "Feeling Groovy" and even a lush a cappella arrangement of "Dixie." In between songs they combined conversational Christian outreach with cheesy one-liners like, "God took a rib out of man and made a loudspeaker."

At intermission Bob Horner, the area director of Campus Crusade, told the audience the group would be playing contemporary Christian folk music after intermission. Almost everyone stayed for a clear musical presentation about how to begin a personal relationship with Jesus.

The campus concert capped an amazing first year at CSM for Walter and Ann. From struggling to put up a poster in his office the first week of class to having his testimony published in the school newspaper, Bible studies with undergraduate fraternity members, undergrad students, and international graduate student couples, along with convincing the student senate to sponsor the New Folk, Walter felt affirmed in his calling to be a Christian professor in ways he never could have imagined. It reminded him of the promise in Jeremiah 29:11: "'For I know the plans I have for you'—this is the Lord's declaration—'plans for your well-being, not for disaster, to give you a future and a hope.'"

Because of the large number of students coming to Christ at CSM, the Bradleys pleaded with CCC area director Bob Horner to send some staff a couple of days a week to help with the follow-up and discipleship. While students at Mines were receptive to the gospel, the six Campus Crusade staff members at the University of Colorado, only nineteen miles north of CSM, had trouble filling their appointment schedules even though the university had twenty-five thousand students. Ray Womack and J. P. Moreland came to assist the Bradleys two days a week. Later Bob Tiede joined the team at Mines as well. Tiede went on to become the primary support staff for Josh McDowell, and J. P. Moreland later earned his PhD in philosophy with Professor Dallas Willard and became a prominent professor at Biola University.

The next seven years at CSM were full of opportunities for Walter and Ann to grow in their faith as they saw God working in ways far beyond what they and their students could have imagined. "Like Daniel and his friends in Babylon," Walter wrote, "God gave us favor in a 'foreign land' with students and faculty alike." During his first year teaching at Mines, Dr. Bradley submitted a proposal for and received a very prestigious Young Investigator Award from the National Science Foundation. Only one YIA proposal in eight was funded by the Foundation during the 1968–69 academic year.

Dr. Bradley started strong at CSM and soon continued his climb up the academic ladder. Fewer than half of the applicants for promotion to associate professor were successful, but he was promoted to associate professor of metallurgical engineering after just three years rather than the usual five. Bradley admitted, "I wasn't the best teacher at CSM my first year there, but I made up with enthusiasm and extra effort what I lacked in experience."

Walter reflected on his time at Mines as an example of Matthew 6:33: "Seek first the kingdom of God and his righteousness, and all these things will be provided for you." Walter and Ann took a big chance investing so much of their time in Christian ministry rather than working the seventy to eighty hours a week typically required of professors seeking tenure. Yet in his first year at CSM, Walter received a university-wide teaching award that was based on student nominations. His students could see how much he cared and how hard he worked to help them succeed, which most did. He was a good example of the saying, "Students don't care how much you know until they know how much you care."

By his eighth year on the faculty, Dr. Bradley would be known as one of the best teachers at the school, earning a second teaching award acknowledging his efforts that year.

In typical fashion, as his professional career gained momentum Dr. Bradley pursued a range of other interests: his family, his students, and his tireless work in the service of Christ.

CHAPTER 4

Adventures at Home and Abroad

In the spring of 1969, the Bradleys and daughter, Sharon, welcomed their newest arrival, Steve, to the family. They finished their new house on the property that Walter bought from his predecessor and moved from faculty apartment housing into their spacious new home. It was the nicest, biggest place they'd ever had, their first house after five years in a series of apartments. In fact, it was so big they didn't have enough furniture to fill it up. The children didn't mind; it gave them more room to play and run around inside.

True to form, Walter saved money at every opportunity by doing maintenance and improvements himself. A swing set and a rock wall were two projects he tackled constructing, sometimes with little Steve tagging along. The wall was about three feet tall, running ninety feet across the front of the house and continuing sixty feet on the side. Walter recently noted, "It looks as good today as it did when it was built fifty years ago."

After a few years, Walter and Ann decided their new home was bigger than they needed, so they moved the family into a smaller home that was less expensive and easier to maintain. The lower living costs made it possible for them to have a date night every week and to tithe to their church without skimping.

The family loved to go skiing. Sharon and Steve learned to ski when they were four and five years old. Years later Steve believed one of the reasons his father was so happy to move to Colorado for his first teaching job was for the skiing. When Dr. Bradley was a student at the University of Texas, his fraternity brothers took skiing trips, but he couldn't afford to join them. Now he could go skiing frequently, with the Loveland ski area less than an hour west of his home in Golden.

As Walter advanced his professional career at Colorado School of Mines, he and Ann developed a two-track system for continuing their Christian outreach: one for faculty and their families and one for students. They kept hosting discussions for interested professors at their apartment while helping to lead Bible studies for students under the umbrella of Campus Crusade for Christ. Students who joined them early on eventually became the leadership of the new Campus Crusade for Christ group at CSM, the first recognized Christian student group in the history of the university.

In 1972, some Christians bought a house across the street from campus and christened it Agape House, after the biblical term *agape*, which means a love based on friendship. They used the house for small Bible studies and fellowship. Soon the space was too small for regular CCC meetings. The Friday-night outreach and fellowship gatherings drew an average of more than a hundred students. Tuesday-night discipleship classes had about sixty. These gatherings—remarkable numbers for a campus of only 1,600 students—were held in meeting rooms on campus.

That year Campus Crusade wove together several threads of popular culture and faith outreach in a phenomenon they named Explo '72. It combined elements of the evangelical Christian movement on campus, the emerging sound of contemporary Christian music, and the huge public rallies popularized by political protests and anti-war demonstrations together for a massive event in Dallas, Texas, that Campus Crusade hoped would mobilize American students for good and inspire Christian revival across the country.

Walter and Ann couldn't stand to watch such a high-profile event from the sidelines. They hosted a busload of students to make the trek from Colorado to Texas, most of whom had become Christians through the Campus Crusade chapter Ann and Walter started.

Explo '72 took place in the Cotton Bowl in Dallas on June 12–17. Every Christian spiritual leader with a national presence was there, along with every Christian musician with a respectable following. It was a Texas-size revival the likes of which haven't been seen before or since. One sultry spring evening there was a demonstration of how each participant could spread the light of Christ. Everyone in the stadium had a candle. Starting with a single candle, candles were lit one at a time until the whole venue flickered and glowed with the light of sixty thousand flames. Nearby residents called the fire department to report the Cotton Bowl was on fire.

The last night of the event was a Christian music concert. Anticipated crowds were so large that organizers moved out of the stadium and onto a huge space that had been cleared and graded for a soon-to-be-built freeway. The concert lasted eight hours. Some commentators labeled it the "Christian Woodstock." Looking back, historians of pop culture mark it as the moment contemporary Christian music came into being.

"It was a life-changing experience for all of us," Walter remembered of the trip. From that group of students, more than ten went into full-time Christian ministry, some for a few years and some until they retired decades later. "Our God just got a lot bigger that week and so did the students' God!" Walter said.

Another Christian movement began in Dallas the same year that paralleled Walter's interest in sharing the message of Christ. In 1973, Jon Buell and Jimmy Williams started Probe Ministries. Their aim was to spread the gospel message on American campuses and connect Christian professors with speaking opportunities at secular colleges. The ministry set up two- or three-day events for professors to speak to skeptical audiences of students and their professors. Probe helped stimulate Walter's lifelong interest in the intersection of faith and science by providing opportunities for him to test the ideas he was developing through careful study of the technical literature on the origin of life and the "fine-tuning" of the universe.

Walter knew that in the first half of the twentieth century, as modern science came into its own with many new remarkable insights such as Schrodinger's quantum mechanics and Einstein's theory of relativity, many secular and some atheist scientists saw science as a way to explain the nature of nature without any reference to a creator God. But in the 1960s and 1970s, new discoveries seemed to challenge a naturalistic explanation for the origin of life.

It was Jon Buell of Probe Ministries, Walter said, who "got me interested in using my background in science to explore questions at the interface between faith and science for my own benefit and to be able to address these questions for others. It was during this time that I began to give talks on thermodynamics and the origin of life. I was pleased to discover, while giving lectures in classes of biochemistry for seniors at secular universities such as the University of Colorado and Colorado State University, that the questions I was raising regarding the thermodynamic obstacles to the origin of life were conceded to be real by the professors of these classes, who had never had these problems brought to their attention partly because their background in physical chemistry was pretty weak."

Based on his scientific study, Walter gradually became convinced that natural laws were completely inadequate to explain the fine-tuning of the universe and the origin of life on earth. No explanation advanced in favor of life beginning as a matter of chance—tidal pools, lightning strikes, chemical soup, clouds of gasses—could overcome the biochemical and thermodynamic obstacles to the origin of life.

For all of his intense pursuit of scientific studies, Walter and Ann remained equally dedicated to sharing their faith one-on-one. By the early 1970s, the impact of their Christian outreach was already immense. The scope of their influence on the lives of students, faculty, friends, and foes over the years is impossible to gauge. Surely thousands of people have embraced Christianity—or at least reconsidered it—because of the Bradleys' courteous, cordial, yet unwavering commitment to sharing their faith.

To get some sense of the difference Walter made, we can let one student's experience represent the many, then multiply it by thousands.

Rich Wilson arrived at Colorado School of Mines in the fall of 1972. He had been through hard times personally, butting heads with his father, a NASA scientist who transferred from the manned space program to NORAD (North American Air Defense Command) in Colorado because Rich "was getting in so much trouble."

Though they didn't know each other at the time, Rich and Dr. Bradley both attended Explo '72, where Rich became a Christian.

Rich's father warned him he'd never be able to get into CSM. Yet Rich squeaked by as the last applicant with the lowest grades to be admitted to the freshman class of 1972–73. The dean cautioned Wilson that he shouldn't expect to graduate. Only one out of three entering freshmen survived all four years. "I already knew I wouldn't make it," Rich recalled.

Rich met Dr. Bradley for the first time at a CCC gathering to welcome incoming freshmen. A Campus Crusade representative visited Rich's dorm to promote the event. When the rep learned Rich was interested in metallurgy, he suggested Rich go to the reception to meet a metallurgical professor named Walter Bradley. Because of their common interest in faith and the science of metals, Rich felt an instant connection with the friendly professor.

Dr. Bradley attended CCC Bible studies and sometimes led them. Rich's impression of Bradley was that "he spent all day working for the school and all night working for us." In those Bible studies Rich learned a lot about the decisions Walter had made as a young Christian. "Dr. Bradley was the one you listened to the most because he was the most intelligent and the most authoritative," Rich commented. "The whole school was science geeks and he was our kind." Bradley understood how to communicate with these young students hungry for spiritual answers.

Rich was enthusiastic about Agape House as a place to get away for quiet study and reflection. There was a key hidden outside so that anyone could go in for Bible study or private prayer. Agape House was open to all Christian organizations, even if they weren't connected with CCC or Colorado School of Mines. Bradley and the other benefactors saw it as a tool for Christian outreach that was not restricted to any one group. When Rich joined a fraternity, he learned Dr. Bradley was teaching a Bible study there. Others also led the studies, but "Dr. Bradley's were always the best."

After about a year, Walter gradually started handing over leadership of the fraternity Bible study to Rich. He gave Rich the slender book he had been teaching out of—*The Ten Basic Steps to Christian Maturity*—a tract written in 1951 by Campus Crusade founder Bill Bright. Dr. Bradley was "more interested in teaching me how to do it than he was to keep doing it himself," Rich said. "I ended up learning as much by teaching as I did by listening."

Rich took his first metallurgy class from Dr. Bradley during his junior year in the fall of 1974. Fairly early in the semester, Rich recalled, the professor delivered his scheduled lecture, then said, "I would like to share with you the most interesting thing to know about me. I am a follower of Jesus Christ, and by that I do not mean that I just go to church on Sundays. It is the very foundation on which everything that I do is built, and I hope that you will see that it makes a difference in how I treat you."

As Rich recalls, initially three-quarters or so of the students stayed after class to see what was happening. Once they realized the topic was Christianity, many left, leaving about a fourth of the class. Eventually that number got down to a small group that then shifted over to the Agape House for a more thorough discussion and question-and-answer time. This core group was truly interested in spiritual ideas.

"Often he would talk about the scientific side of the Bible," Rich said. "For example, he would show that dating the age of the universe scientifically gave a value of approximately fourteen billion. He would then show them that the Hebrew word *yom* can mean 'day' (twelve hours). It can also mean a calendar day, twenty-four hours, or even an indeterminate period of time, which is surely the intent in Genesis 1–3. He would also give lectures on fine-tuning of the universe on the origin of life. When I figured out what he was talking about, it was like, wow!"

Dr. Bradley taught that God had revealed himself in two "books": His written revelation in the Bible and His physical revelation in the created world for everyone to see His majesty, power, love, and provision for them. Bradley also showed that the more we learn through the eyes of science, the more we see a universe that cannot be the result of cosmic accidents.

Along with other students, Rich often went to the professor's house for Bible studies. He got to know Ann and eventually started going to the church the Bradleys attended. On the academic front, Bradley noticed that, as predicted, Rich was having trouble with his grades and was soon struggling to hold on to a C average. Professor Bradley called Rich into his office one day and showed him his latest test paper. This, Bradley declared, was unacceptable. Rich was to come to his office every Thursday evening from five thirty until six for one-on-one tutoring. As payment, Rich had to babysit the Bradley children. Rich readily accepted the offer and soon raised his grade. "When I realized he was paying attention," Rich said, "it embarrassed me and I caught up pretty quick."

The first time Rich went to the Bradley house to babysit, Walter took him into the backyard to introduce him to the children. There he got a firsthand look at one of Walter's discipline techniques. Steve and Sharon were in the backyard fighting over a candy bar. Walter got their attention and said that one of the kids could break the candy bar in two. The result was one piece about twice the size of the other. Then the other child got first choice of the halves. The one in charge of splitting the treat was shocked to tears.

One story Rich recalled illustrates the ripple effect of Walter's eagerness to share his faith. According to Rich, the vice president of his fraternity blackballed him because he was a Christian. Rich and his Christian classmates invited this fraternity brother to a Bible study on how to accept Christ. It didn't have any effect on him at the time. But at the end of the summer, during a camping trip with some of the other students in the study, lightning hit a tree above their heads. In front of them all, this former skeptic got down on his knees and prayed to receive Christ.

He died the next week. Decades later, tears still welled up in Rich Wilson's eyes as he told the story.

Though Walter left CSM after Rich's junior year, the two of them stayed in touch. To Rich, his metallurgy professor and Bible teacher has been like a second father. He especially remembers Walter's support at key moments in his life: his divorce, his father's death, the birth of his son.

"I became a successful metallurgist, made several breakthroughs, and ran my own company," Rich reported. "With my dad gone, Walter still fulfills that supporting role. When my grandson was born with an arm problem, I met with Dr. Bradley several times just to discuss it."

Other students from Walter's years at CSM have kept in touch as well. In 2012, a group of alumni contacted him to say they wanted to organize a reunion. About forty people, many of whom hadn't seen each other since the 1970s, got together to relive their early Christian experience and honor the man who had encouraged and guided them.

"We had such a great time," the Bradleys recently recalled. "The people who were there were now grown-up men and women who had grandchildren. And they were following Christ, their kids were following Christ, and they had grandchildren whom they were also trying to see become Christians. You plant the little mustard seed thinking it's going to be insignificant and then it grows into this big, huge tree. We had thirteen kids majoring in engineering during the eight years we were at CSM who went into some kind of full-time Christian work."

Dr. Bradley continued, "CSM is a very different campus today. It used to be spiritually dark, and today it seems to be spiritually very, very light. It's nice to have the privilege of starting something and then seeing it go on to even bigger and better things, which is just to say it wasn't my ministry, it was God's ministry. He was perfectly capable of taking good care of it when we were there and perfectly capable of taking good care of it when we left."

During his time at the Colorado School of Mines, Dr. Bradley developed what he called "a significant interest in faith and science questions, partly in response to my own curiosity and partly because when people learned that I was a Christian and a professor/doctor of materials science and engineering, I got lots of questions, especially from my students at CSM, particularly those of the CCC student group."

With his promotion to associate professor and his professional career off to an excellent start, he began investing more of his extracurricular ministry time in faith-science questions. In 1973, he joined the American Scientific Affiliation, an international organization of Christians in the sciences. ASA describes itself as a forum for an open and honest discussion of the relationship between Christianity and science. According to their website, members of the ASA "believe that God is both the creator of our vast universe and is the source of our ability to pursue knowledge," accepting both orthodox Christianity and mainstream science. Their journal, *Perspectives on Science and Christian Faith*, publishes only high-quality, peer-reviewed articles and has national and regional conferences to address these topics.

The same year Dr. Bradley joined ASA, his friend and Probe Ministries co-founder Jon Buell invited him to write a book on faith and science.

Buell originally suggested a book on evolution, but Walter deferred, as he had no background in biology, much less evolutionary biology. Dr. Bradley countered with a suggestion that he explore the origin of life to see if there were significant unanswered questions in this area and if his background in polymers, chemical kinetics, and chemical thermodynamics was suitable to explore the answers. Bradley's preliminary investigation into the origin of life literature convinced him that there were important unanswered questions and that his background in polymer science and engineering was well suited to look into them.

Dr. Bradley's professional affiliation with ASA and his encouragement from Probe Ministries to write at length on the origin of life would lead, more than a decade later, to one of the most important and influential projects of his career. In the meantime, there were other adventures at hand.

Dr. Bradley had a PhD student from Brazil, Carlos Coutinho, who moved his wife and two children to Colorado for the three years it took to earn his degree. Carlos and his wife went to a Bible study Walter and Ann hosted for graduate students and their wives. As Carlos prepared to go home to Brazil, he asked Dr. Bradley if he would accept a six-month teaching contract there if Carlos could arrange it. Thinking it was highly unlikely, Walter said he would be happy to come.

Two months later, on New Year's Day 1974, Carlos called to say, "Happy New Year. You have a teaching and consulting contract with FIMA!" The offer was a six-month contract from March through August as a consultant to this government agency whose responsibility was to help Brazilian industry be more competitive in the global market as well as in Brazil. Dr. Bradley would teach one graduate class in materials science and engineering at the Federal Technical University in Minas Gerais and provide consulting services to the government on the steel industry. Brazilian officials wanted someone for the job who had no previous relationship with the universities or steel companies so that the recommendations would be free of political bias.

For a thirty-one-year-old college professor, this was a remarkable opportunity: six months of paid travel to all of the major universities and steel companies in Brazil. Yet there were plenty of practical reasons not to make the trip. First was that the Bradleys' children were just starting school. Sharon was in the first grade and Steve was in kindergarten. If they moved, the family would live in Belo Horizonte, a city of one and a half million people five hours inland, where there were no English schools. The Bradley children would have to be dropped cold turkey into Portuguese-speaking classrooms.

The second practical problem was Walter's spring teaching schedule. He had two classes and couldn't abandon them in the middle of the term. He told Carlos he would ask his department head about the opportunity, secretly hoping the answer would be no. Walter's department head surprised him by saying not only that he could go but that he thought it was a great idea. All Walter had to do was get substitutes to teach his classes.

Much to his amazement, the first two colleagues he asked were willing to help him. Each would turn one of their classes over to Walter the first half of the semester, then teach one of his classes the last half of the term. This meant that until he left, Walter would teach his own two courses three times a week plus three lectures each week for his colleagues' two classes. Twelve lectures each week, including six on unfamiliar material, made for a grueling schedule. However, he happily shouldered the load for the opportunity it meant.

The third problem was financial. The offer from Brazil included all Walter's American salary for six months plus travel expenses, but no money for the family's travel costs and living expenses. Walter's department head decided that since Walter was doing a semester's worth of teaching in half a semester, he would pay Walter's whole spring salary upfront. That gave Walter enough money to bring his wife and children.

As plans for moving to Brazil unfolded, Walter also forged ahead with a major campus-wide outreach for CCC. He and Ann asked if the organization would host an appearance by André Kole, a renowned illusionist who had become a Christian and shared his story on large campuses across the country. Kole was famous for offering a $1 million prize to anyone who could perform a supernatural miracle in his presence under controlled conditions (the prize remains unclaimed). Remarkably, he had one open date during his time in Colorado in February 1974.

CCC students got permission to use the newly completed 1,400-seat auditorium for Kole's appearance rather than the student cafeteria that seated only 250, hoping they could draw a respectable crowd. By the date of the event, the 60 discipleship students had sold 20 tickets each for a total of 1,200 or 75 percent of the student body.

André Kole mesmerized the audience performing one feat after another that truly looked like supernatural miracles. Just before intermission, Kole explained that what seemed to be supernatural was only a series of clever illusions, and that during the second half he would talk about the truly supernatural works of Jesus. To Walter's astonishment, no one left at intermission. Instead, the entire audience heard a powerful presentation of the gospel.

For Ann and Walter, this night was the culmination of an impossible dream. They had arrived at CSM five and a half years earlier to discover that there was no organized Christian activity on campus. Now tonight, more than three-fourths of the campus at once was soaking up a compelling Christian message.

Walter said, "I remember Ann and me crying tears of joy as we watched this miracle unfolding before our very eyes that evening. It was the fulfillment of the promise that 'we never test the resources of God until we attempt the impossible.' This was the beginning of the fulfillment of this promise over and over again in our lives."

Only a month later the Bradleys were on their way to Brazil. The first challenge on their journey was their fourteen suitcases. At the ticket counter the Bradleys learned that their luggage surcharge would be between $600 and $700, as anything over forty-four pounds of luggage per passenger cost an extra three dollars a pound. Walter explained that if that was the case, they would have to leave ten bags behind. They were going to Brazil so he could teach, and he didn't have the cash to cover this amount (credit cards were relatively rare then). After listening to his story, the agent waved the family and their mountain of luggage through with no extra charge.

Their relief was short-lived. Walter had scheduled a two-day stopover in Caracas, Venezuela, to visit another former student. When they returned to the airport to continue their trip, they faced the luggage surcharge problem all over again. The gate agent wasn't sure about the policy in Caracas for extra baggage so he asked how much the New York agent had charged. When Walter said there had been no extra cost, the Caracas agent didn't charge them either. They took off once more for Rio, then took a commuter flight to Belo Horizonte.

Though there was an American neighborhood in the city, Walter didn't want his family to miss the excitement of living in a foreign community. Also, an apartment in the American enclave was $900 per month, compared to $200 elsewhere. Walter never could resist a bargain, even though life among the locals meant a building with no hot water and electrical outages an average of twice a day. But it did give the Bradleys an opportunity to experience living like a middle-class Brazilian family.

One of the first hurdles was the language barrier. Belo had a population of 1.5 million people with only 150 native English speakers. Ann was able to convert her Spanish into Portuguese, and Walter took Portuguese two nights a week and eventually could speak "like an intelligent five- or six-year-old." Walter taught his graduate course in English, which the students could read but not easily speak, resulting in a lot of handouts in English for each class.

As planned, Walter also visited major steel companies across the country identifying problems in materials quality and/or production. He visited every major university as well, then wrote a report matching steel company research needs with university capabilities. The government would then fund research projects at the various campuses based on Dr. Bradley's recommendations.

One interesting aspect of the assignment was the chance to visit competing steel companies and learn details about their operations. "In America one steel company wouldn't want me learning their secrets and then going to visit the competition," Walter said. But he was careful never to divulge trade secrets of any company to its competitors.

Walter and Ann quickly began looking for ways to keep sharing their faith. They found a Baptist church in Belo Horizonte and soon made friends there. The senior pastor had been to a Campus Crusade for Christ conference and was very excited to apply what he had learned. The church was eager to have Ann and Walter working with their youth group of eighty teenagers, but the language barrier was a potential challenge. Providentially, a church family that had lived in the United States for two years had four children in the youth group who spoke perfect English and were happy to translate.

While Walter and Ann adjusted well to their new surroundings, Sharon and Steve didn't have much fun. They had a rough time learning Portuguese, and by the time they started to feel comfortable with the language it was time to return home. Still, according to Walter, it was "a family adventure that was pretty cool. However, we asked Sharon and Steve if they would like to come back another time and they both quickly said no, and that they'd rather stay with their grandparents." Carlos and Dirce Coutinho were wonderful hosts for their six-month visit, and the Bradleys were pleased some years later to have them come to Texas A&M University for nine months for Carolos to teach as a visiting professor.

As Dr. Bradley finished his project and prepared his report for the Brazilian government, he started planning his family's return to Colorado. He learned that he had to go to the police station for clearance to leave the country. When he asked how the police knew he was there, Carlos explained, "When you registered at the police station when you got here, they kept a record of your entry. When you apply to leave, they will make sure you have no outstanding fines or other legal matters."

"But we didn't know we were supposed to register at the police station!" Walter said. Carlos showed him the entry stamp in his passport. Walter hadn't read it since it was in Portuguese. It said he and his family were required to register with the police within two weeks of their arrival. The fine for failing to register was $10 a day per person. The fine was so large—$7,300—the university had to take its appeal all the way to the office of the president of Brazil to get a waiver. Fortunately, since he was working on a government contract, the government was willing to waive the fine.

As another way to save money, Walter had decided to buy a used Volkswagen bug and furniture in Brazil and then sell them when they left. What he didn't know was that although he could bring any amount of United States currency into Brazil, he could only take out the equivalent of $300. Here was yet another money dilemma. How would they be able to return with the eight thousand dollars' worth of Brazilian *cruzeiros* that Walter had after he sold his car, his furniture, and received his last paycheck from the Brazilian government?

Once again the Bradleys' guardian angel stepped in. A missionary family from Iowa had not been allowed to cash their expense and payroll checks at a local bank in Brazil because their mission organization was delayed in depositing their moving and payroll check for two months. Walter offered to sell the missionaries his *cruzeiros* for a postdated check on their bank back home. The grateful missionaries were astonished that God provided strangers who would take a postdated check on a bank half-way around the world. The Bradleys were similarly amazed that God had provided a way for them to get the $8,000 out of Brazil. Walter and his family returned to the United States and two months later were able to successfully cash the check.

Looking back on the experience, Walter was grateful for the professional opportunity, the chance to share his foreign adventure with his family, and the unexpected openings to teach the Bible to a room full of Brazilian teenagers. They were blessed by one wonderful miracle after another. Not the least of which was that in six months no one in the family had a single day of the stomach distress that so often affected Americans in their foreign travel.

PART TWO

In Full Flower

1976–2003

His education complete and his professional course firmly set, Dr. Walter Bradley returned to Texas and took on the challenge of joining, and eventually leading, the largest university mechanical engineering department in the country.

For more than two decades at Texas A&M, Dr. Bradley's work on campus represented the output of a busy, accomplished, and successful man. But his academic and engineering interests, enough to keep any other ambitious professor running to the point of exhaustion, are only part of the story.

Dr. Bradley served for four years as department head and held other distinguished professional positions on and off campus. He also gained national renown as an author and one of the earliest voices to describe and defend the concept of intelligent design. At the same time, Walter and Ann raised two children; opened their home almost constantly to friends, neighbors, students, and strangers alike for discussions, Bible studies, and more; served faithfully in their church; and organized and funded a crisis pregnancy support center. Dr. Bradley also gained a nationwide reputation as a consultant and expert witness, his gentlemanly manner giving way to iron resolve in the face of aggressive and duplicitous lawyers.

Walter and his son, Steve, built successful businesses together as engineering consultants in real estate and developed a seminar program for college students called Success4Students.

These were years of a life, a career, and a faith journey in full flower—until God sent the Bradleys in a new direction.

CHAPTER 5

Planting Seeds, Opening Doors

Back on campus in Colorado as the new school year began in the fall of 1974, Dr. Bradley continued to refine his thinking about building an academic career as a Christian. He would not use Christianity as an excuse or a justification to compromise his professional standards. For example, he wouldn't spend less time on an engineering project because he had to go to Bible study. Rather, Christian precepts would always spur him on to greater achievement. He lived out his belief that Christians should strive to be the best at whatever they do.

Dr. Bradley developed a conference presentation for Christian as well as secular audiences on the research and publishing that professors must do if they expect to move up the academic ladder. He identified three possible perspectives: one to avoid and two to embrace by Christian professors.

First, the *cynical view* sees publishing as a meaningless game required by the academy to avoid perishing. Second, the *Christian stewardship view* holds that the time, and sometimes money, made available to academics for their scholarly pursuits carries an obligation to make discoveries and share them with the public, who ultimately pays, either directly or indirectly, for their research opportunities. Third, the *Christian love view* suggests that as professors expand the bounds of knowledge, God may give them significant insights that they should share with other people to make their lives better and enhance their appreciation of God's creation and His goodness. "I am highly motivated if I think of my research and writing as an integral part of how I can serve God by serving His people and helping them to be blessed materially and/or to see God more clearly," Walter wrote.

During his eight years at CSM, Walter took his own advice, becoming a leader in the field of metallurgy. He secured research funding to study fatigue-enhanced creep in aluminum and its alloys from the National Science Foundation and Alcoa Aluminum. Along with colleague assistant professor David Olson and later, assistant professor David Matlock, he received funding from the Department of Energy to study the effect of liquid lithium on stainless steel. The paper that resulted from this work was honored as the Best Materials Paper of 1978 by the American Nuclear Society.

By then, however, Dr. Bradley had left Colorado for the chance to serve God and advance his career in a much larger arena.

In the spring of 1976, Walter Bradley was offered a faculty position at Texas A&M in mechanical engineering. It was a difficult choice. Mines was more highly ranked for its study of metallurgy, but Texas A&M was a much larger school and well known for its mechanical engineering department.

In the summer of 1976, Walter Bradley resigned from the Colorado School of Mines to take the job at Texas A&M University in College Station, Texas. He had been looking for a chance to return to Texas because his and Ann's parents were getting older. He wanted them to be able to spend more time with the grandchildren, who were then seven and eight years old. But the change had huge risks professionally, and it meant leaving his one hundred CCC students.

To encourage Dr. Bradley to stay, the Colorado School of Mines promised him an early promotion to full professor, after only eight years at Mines. It was a clear signal that he had excelled professionally and honored Christ in his work. Despite the offer, Walter and Ann decided he should accept the new position in Texas. After a week of intensive prayer, they were hopeful they would have another great opportunity for ministry at TAMU, but it would be entirely different, as there were already six full-time CCC staff at A&M.

Walter Bradley in 1976.

While this move was motivated by family considerations, it proved to be the most important decision of his academic and ministry careers. From an academic standpoint, Texas A&M was a fruitful place to research plastic and polymeric composites. Bradley's good friend Dr. Richard Schapery encouraged him in the field and invited him to join him in this new area, "harvesting in an almost empty orchard." On the ministry side, there were many new opportunities to work with Christian professors and spouses while letting the healthy campus organizations minister to Aggie students. From their experience at Mines, Ann and Walter knew how effective Christian professors could be in reinforcing and sharing their message of faith.

The Bradleys believed the Lord would take care of the "spiritual children" they left behind in Colorado. Today there are three major Christian ministries at CSM: Cru, the new name of Campus Crusade for Christ; Intervarsity Christian Fellowship; and the Navigators. As Walter observed, "God used the small seeds that we planted to grow the biggest tree in the garden." Mines today is very welcoming to Christian groups and their influence.

The Bradley family moved from Golden, Colorado, to College Station in August. Consistent with his frugal nature, Walter rented a fourteen-foot

U-Haul covered trailer to transport some of their household goods himself. The family left Golden midday without making a hotel reservation for the night because Walter didn't know how far they would get by bedtime while pulling the trailer. He hoped to drive as far as Amarillo, Texas, which they reached about 10:00 p.m.

As Walter recalled, "Every motel in Amarillo was full. There were motorcycles everywhere—we had landed in the middle of a biker rally." Unfazed, Walter and his family continued down the road. "We went through the next two small towns, whose motels were also full. After the third town and still no vacancies, we pulled into the parking lot of a Walmart. I dragged a mattress out of the trailer. Steve and I slept there, and Ann and Sharon slept in the car. We had a reasonably restful night except for the eighteen-wheelers roaring by the whole time. When Walmart customers started showing up the next morning, I hurriedly packed up the mattress and we continued on our way."

One of the changes the Bradleys anticipated in leaving the Rocky Mountains was having to give up their weekend ski trips. While living in Golden, Walter and Ann had taken every advantage of the nearby opportunities to ski. Three years before the move to Texas, they had decided it was time for the children's first skiing lessons. They all went to Lake Eldora just west of Boulder because it had an easy beginner's run.

Walter remembered, "I gave the kids some lessons at the bottom of the beginner's hill and then we took the chair to the top. At the top of the hill they asked where the restrooms were. Well, there weren't any up there. I told them to just go in their pants. To make matters worse, they filled their waterproof ski boots with pee. It was a disastrous first ski trip. This completely freaked them out and they said they'd never go skiing again! When we took them back next season, our first stop was the restroom.

"Steve and Sharon both developed into excellent skiers, and skiing became our favorite family activity. When we decided to move to College Station, I promised them we'd take a skiing vacation to Colorado every Christmas, which we did."

The 1970s marked a historic season of change for the automotive industry. New federal safety, fuel efficiency, and clean-air regulations had carmakers scurrying for answers: five-mile-per-hour bumpers, catalytic converters and the phase-out of leaded gasoline, a legal battle over air bags, and much more. In 1977, Goodyear predicted that by the mid-1980s about 85 percent of the typical family car would be made of rubber or plastic. The same year the chairman of Inland Steel figured carmakers would trim seven hundred pounds from the average car by substituting other materials for steel. Ford Motor Company announced it was adding more than half a million square feet of factory space to make plastic parts to replace metal instrument panels, fuel tanks, grilles, and other components. The company also planned to make an experimental car out of carbon fiber, reducing the weight of the same car made with steel by 1,250 pounds.

"In 1977, I read that Ford Motor Company hoped to make its automobiles almost entirely out of plastics and composites by the year 2000. It was this article that created my interest in making a major career change toward engineering plastics and composites, ramping down my work in metals and alloys."

As the industry moved into this new chapter of auto manufacturing, there were big questions to consider. How strong and reliable were plastics and other lightweight alternatives compared with steel? How long would they last, and when would they fail? What changes would the manufacturing processes have to undergo to accommodate them? Carmakers around the world needed lots of new information as they made the huge and complicated pivot away from steel toward lightweight alternatives. Dr. Walter Bradley resolved to be one of the first experts who could supply them with answers.

The news about coming changes in the automotive industry "planted the seed that plastics and polymeric composites would be a dynamic new field of materials science and engineering," Walter later said. "I did not do much immediately, but was invited in 1978 by my colleague Dr. Dick Schapery, who also went to Grace Bible Church where Ann and I attended, to be part of his proposal to the Air Force for a center to do research on high-performance graphite-epoxy composite materials that could have the strength of steel at less than 33 percent of the weight—ideal for jet fighters and other military applications and also of keen interest to NASA, who is always trying to trim weight from their launches.

"Dr. Schapery invited me to join his team of five professors. Eventually the Air Force funded five years of our research. Through this involvement, I was able to become established as a major player in this new field, which meant I was able to get an abundance of research funding for the next fifteen years with modest effort. I was subsequently invited to do research with NASA and then for various Fortune 500 companies like DuPont, Dow Chemical, and 3M in this emerging new area, all because of the jump start I got working with Dr. Schapery."

Bradley and Schapery developed a new method to measure the resistance of various carbon fiber–reinforced epoxies or other materials to delamination. Beyond measuring resistance to crack growth between plies of the carbon-reinforced epoxies, Dr. Bradley's research group was the first to publish high-magnification pictures taken in a scanning electron microscope specially equipped with a mechanical stage to load the test samples until they began to delaminate. Was the crack initiation due to manufacturing defects in the graphite-epoxy composite, an interfacial fracture between the fibers and their surrounding epoxy, or the failure of the epoxy matrix itself? These observations guided the creation of very stiff and highly reliable graphite-epoxy composite components in air force fighter jets.

Dr. Bradley also pursued numerous other areas of research. Early in his career he became interested in a new technique for measuring the resistance of materials to crack growth, the J-integral approach. Using this new methodology, he demonstrated that ductile cast iron had a much higher resistance to crack growth than had been predicted by Charpy impact testing, the current standard at the time. This insight opened up new areas of opportunity for research into nodular cast iron. In 2019 he received a call from an engineer who read his work published in 1984 and was trying to decide if he could safely use ductile cast iron.

In another area of polymer science and engineering, Dr. Bradley established an international reputation for his pioneering work in lifetime prediction of internally pressurized plastic pipe. Toward the end of the twentieth century, residential and commercial builders began replacing cast-iron water pipes with plastic pipe in new construction. While cast iron had a well-established reputation for durability, lasting more than fifty years in many applications, plastic pipe was much cheaper to purchase and install. But how long would plastic pipe last? The challenge was to design a materials model and test strategy that could reliably predict the service life of plastic pipe over thirty years or more using tests that could be completed in one to two years.

Plastic pipe manufacturers used accelerated testing over six to eighteen months to predict how well their pipe would perform over a product lifetime. Using plastic pipe to distribute hot tap water was problematic because chlorine, even in the concentration of a few parts per million, can degrade plastic pipe over time.

Dr. Bradley initially got involved in this challenging question of plastic pipe durability as an expert witness for the DuPont Chemical Company in a $2 billion class action lawsuit. Shell Chemical had developed a new plastic for residential plumbing and predicted a service life of more than thirty-plus years based on accelerated testing. It went on the market in the early 1980s and was an immediate commercial success. Unfortunately, the pipe began to fail after only eight years in service, requiring replacement in many homes. As Dr. Bradley explained, "It was my job to determine whether the primary cause of failure was the pipe made with a Shell plastic or the fittings made with a DuPont plastic, and to determine why the life prediction was so incorrect.

"The result of my failure-analysis work established that the Shell Chemical plastic in the pipe was the primary cause of these pipe failures around the country. Working with my son, Steven, we were able to determine why the life predictions were so inaccurate." Shell eventually paid a $925 million settlement and left the plastic pipe business.

Through the work that Dr. Bradley and his son did in this case and in another multimillion-dollar lawsuit against General Electric for a plastic they sold to makers of in-line water heaters, the two consultants developed a significantly improved life-prediction protocol for plastics used in hot chlorinated water. Their seminal research became key additions to a new American Society for Testing and Materials (ASTM) test standard for life prediction of plastic pipe. Walter noted, "This new standard was instrumental in guiding the development of plastic pipe that today is widely accepted in residential applications and can last thirty years or more."

In recognition of his work in time-dependent crack growth in plastics and polymeric composites, Dr. Bradley was honored by an invitation to write an article for the first volume of a new journal, *Mechanics of Time-Dependent Materials.*

Other research yielded results that drove crucial decisions even decades later. Bradley's seminal work to reconcile the different predictions from notched Charpy impact test and fatigue pre-cracked J-integral test to determine the resistance to crack growth in nodular cast iron led to an invitation to write a state-of-the-art paper in the journal *International Materials Reviews.* This prestigious publication produces only four issues per year with only four invited papers per issue. As evidence of the enduring importance of this work, Dr. Bradley received a call from a scientist at Westinghouse in 2019 who was using Bradley's paper, published in 1984, to help make a decision on whether it was safe to make shipping containers for transport of nuclear waste out of nodular cast iron rather than cast steel.

Dr. Bradley's renown as an expert witness added further luster to his teaching and research credentials. He was also selected to be a research fellow of the Texas A&M University Engineering Experiment Station (TEES, the research organization of the College of Engineering) in 1980 in recognition of his research. In 1985, he became a Senior Fellow, an honor that was renewed annually for the fifteen years he remained a faculty member at Texas A&M. In 1986, Bradley became director of the TEES Polymer Technology Center, which he helped establish to conduct applied research in collaboration with the plastics industry in high-performance polymers and polymeric composites.

He later recalled, "During my twenty-four years at Texas A&M University, I was allowed to do up to one day a week of consulting if it related to my teaching and/or research. The benefit to the university was that my teaching and research were enhanced with real, current case studies. I also published numerous case studies in refereed journals and conference proceedings on failure analysis and product liability involving metals and plastics. Needless to say, my students loved having my teaching enriched with real-world examples. I taught a one-semester elective class on failure analysis and product liability to mechanical engineering students; two of them became directors of large, successful failure analysis firms in Texas."

As Dr. Bradley turned his professional interest to failure analysis and high-strength composites after arriving at Texas A&M, he and Ann turned their spiritual attention to Grace Bible Church. It was a dynamic young congregation with strong ties to the A&M community. Only four years after its organization in 1961, Grace established a Sunday school on campus. The church's focus on Bible exposition appealed to members of the Navigators and Campus Crusade for Christ, so that a sizeable percentage of the congregation were students. A new church building was completed in 1976, the first of a series of new buildings to open as the congregation grew year after year. One of the main reasons Walter and Ann joined Grace was its goal of welcoming the university community and encouraging students to become spiritual leaders both in their fields and in their home communities.

The new and much larger student body and faculty at A&M as compared with CSM gave Walter and Ann more opportunities to reach out to others. They'd learned from their experiences in Colorado, and now they could put that knowledge to use on a broader stage as well as try new ideas. Unlike CSM, which had no student Christian organizations when the Bradleys arrived, A&M already had a number of university-recognized Christian groups on campus. It was a far more Christian-oriented and churchgoing community than the city of Golden had been.

Walter felt that he and Ann had "big open doors to reach out to faculty, both to non-Christian and Christian professors, and also to try to build a community within the Christian faculty group where people could grow in their personal relationship with Jesus and feel more comfortable being identified as one of His followers. If they had a bunch of co-sojourners with them then they were going to feel a little bit more comfortable to be open about their faith."

As he had at CSM, Walter used the student newspaper at A&M, the *Battalion*, to reach out to the campus at large. True to form, he took a confident but nonconfrontational approach that encouraged others to join in supporting the message. A group of professors agreed to chip in the cost and add their signatures to a full-page ad for an informal group who called themselves the Christian Faculty Network at Texas A&M University. As Walter explained, "The ad made a clear but very simple statement of their Christian faith and an invitation to visit personally with students or professors who would like to know more about how they had come to such a belief or conviction." Though there were numerous Christian professors at A&M, many of them "were really, really reluctant to put their name on an ad in the newspaper that they realized everybody was going to see." Even so, Walter had a better start than he'd had at CSM, where only one other colleague had been willing to be identified publicly as a Christian.

"Twenty-four of us did it," Dr. Bradley observed of the ad at A&M, "and nobody got fired, nobody got hassled. People may have talked about us behind our backs, but I'm okay with that. If I don't hear it, I don't care. Even if I do hear it, I don't care. I do occasionally hear skeptical responses from my faculty colleagues to my face, but I still welcome the opportunity to engage in spirited discussion of the veracity of the Christian truth claims."

As a student, Walter had wondered whether Christianity was intellectually acceptable in the scientific and engineering world because he saw so few people around him who identified publicly as Christians. His experience since then taught him that there are Christians who are scientists even though they may hesitate to share their faith. Though only twenty-four professors signed on to that first invitation in the *Battalion*, as the group published similar ads four more times that year, gradually more professors felt comfortable having their names included. Walter explained, "At the beginning there was this feeling that, well, nobody's doing it so it must be inappropriate. Well, no. It's just that nobody had done it."

Walter and his friends had fun with the ads. He said, "Sometimes at Christmas we would put cute ads in there that I'm sure irritated some people, like, 'Wise men still follow Him.' Our aim wasn't to irritate our non-Christian friends but just to make a point with a little humor where possible."

Those early ads set the stage for a broader spiritual presence on campus. Walter said, "What we were able to do at Texas A&M became a great poster child for what's possible. It's great to get faculty together to study the Word, pray together, and support each other. But it's a real shame to just stop at that. Our faculty group at Texas A&M eventually petitioned for and were given formal recognition as The Christian Faculty Network at Texas A&M University." But that success was still years in the future.

Of the sixty or so faculty members in the mechanical engineering department, around fifteen taped the ads to their office doors. Walter's department head, a Jewish agnostic, was extremely upset and embarrassed by this. He complained to the legal office, which told him displaying the ads was perfectly legal. Learning that, he tried to block them in various other ways.

True to form, Walter faced the situation simply and directly, courteous but steadfast in his position. "I know you're the one who's trying to prevent us from putting our ads on our doors," Walter told his department head. "We should go have a long breakfast and talk about it." And they did—for three hours. At the end of their discussion the department head admitted, "You know, I never thought of it that way."

Walter explained that though he had never met a Christian professor during his years at the University of Texas, it was common for professors to ridicule Christians in class. He emphasized that he went into teaching because he wanted to be visible to his students in a way nobody was for him. He told his department head that it wasn't fair to hinder his effort. "You don't know what it's like to be persecuted at the university today. You can be gay, you can be lesbian, you can be almost anything and it's politically incorrect to persecute you," Walter pointed out. "But if you're a Christian it's open season."

"At TAMU we make a concerted effort to hire women professors," Dr. Bradley said. "We look to hire African American professors, Hispanic professors, gay professors, and so forth, to provide role models for all students whatever their background and belief system. How odd it would be not to provide visible role models for students with a religious background."

He further explained that to muzzle only Christian professors violated both Texas state law and the First Amendment. Clearly atheists on campus self-identified and proselytized—the first being fine and the second beyond inappropriate.

"I fully intend to be visible to my students, and it's perfectly legal," Dr. Bradley told the department head. "If it will make you feel any better I will

Find life confusing?
Even a compass needs the North Pole.

Jesus said, "I am the light of the world; he who follows Me shall not walk in the darkness, but will have the light of life." John 8:12.

And now here's the really good news:
God is reaching out to men and women through His son, Jesus Christ. To find out more about God's relevance in your life, We encourage you to read this free article by Josh McDowell: **Does Christianity Work?**
www.leaderu.com/everystudent/josh/josh.html

CHRISTIAN FACULTY

Leaves Heaven for You!

The Christmas Story: The Creator-God of the universe, Jesus Christ, left His home in heaven to become a human being. He lived a perfect life, performed miracles, was betrayed, and wrongfully condemned to death. After being crucified, Jesus' body was placed in a tomb. Three days later, he rose from the dead. After His resurrection, he remained on earth speaking to people for 40 days and then ascended to heaven. Jesus sacrificed himself to make a way for all people to have eternal life in heaven.

Jesus said, "I am the light of the world; he who follows Me shall not walk in darkness, but will have the light of life." -John 8:12. God is reaching out to men and women through His son, Jesus Christ. To find out more about God's relevance in your life, we encourage you to read this article by Josh McDowell: Does Christianity Work? at www.leaderu.com/everystudent/josh/josh.html.

CHRISTIAN FACULTY

These are examples of ads run by the Christian faculty at Texas A&M University in the university newspaper *The Battalion*. Below the words "Christian Faculty" in each ad is written, "We are a group of professors, instructors, lecturers, and administrators united by our common experience that Jesus Christ provides intellectually and spiritually satisfying answers to life's most important questions. We are available to students, faculty, and staff who might like to discuss such questions with us. For more information about the Christian Faculty network and its activities, please visit our website: http://christianfaculty.tamu.edu." Following the message are up to 230 names of Christians on the Texas A&M campus. The practice of publishing such ads began in 1980 when Walter Bradley was able to garner only 23 names.
Ads courtesy of Dr. Micah J. Green, Texas A&M University, micah.green @tamu.edu.

put my advertisement on the inside of my door instead of the outside so that people will see it as they leave, not as they come in." In the end, Walter left his ad where it was and the harassment from that source stopped.

"What's laughable about this," Walter said, "is that at Texas A&M at this time there were fifty-four recognized student Christian groups on campus. The student activities office was well aware that while the university couldn't sponsor these groups, they certainly could permit them just as they permit other affinity groups. Whenever we were told we couldn't exercise our faith we always won the argument. But it goes to show that if you're going to do what God wants you to do on campus you're going to have pushback. You're going to get some guff—some of it from people who are ignorant of what the law says and some are just hateful bullies."

Walter's deans of engineering complained about his expressions of Christianity only five times in his twenty-four years at A&M. It was amazing to him how faithful God was during that season of his life. "If we were willing to take little steps of faith he would do huge things in return. We hoped for little result and blessings on the things we were doing and God would come through and do something far beyond what we expected. It reminded us to just be faithful, step back, and watch God work."

The tradition Bradley started of an ad signed by Christian faculty inviting students to learn more about their faith continues today in the *Battalion* four times a year. The list of signatures has grown over the years to 250 faculty members from all over campus, including many of the most outstanding and accomplished professors. As Walter noted, "Now you can read that ad and say, 'Wow, it's okay to be a Christian at this school. Look at all the faculty, particularly some of the most outstanding faculty, who are Christian!'"

This small seed eventually helped to spur a campus-wide shift in attitude. Today Christianity maintains a powerful presence on campus. As Bradley pointed out, "Texas A&M is the only school I know of that will have a campus-wide Tuesday-night worship and then a Bible lesson, and all the student Christian groups come together for that. They'll have between three and six thousand students every week. It's not just because they're a very visible Christian faculty group. But there's no doubt in my mind that it became much easier for the Christian kids to be identified to their non-Christian friends as Christians, to feel like that if there are this many of the outstanding professors that are Christians it must be intellectually okay."

Along with strengthening the Christian presence on campus, Walter and Ann looked for opportunities to do good in the town of College Station. When they arrived, the couple was very concerned about the growing practice of abortion. It was incredible to them that a college town the size of this one had no crisis pregnancy support resources. Even the most basic services were scarce in the community. Home pregnancy tests were not easy to get in the 1980s, and there was a stigma attached even to buying them. The Bradleys wanted to help start a crisis pregnancy center by finding financial supporters and someone to spearhead the day-to-day services. They needed a volunteer who would take charge of recruiting a like-minded board and some counselors, but no one was willing. "Finally, by default," Walter recalled, "Ann and I decided reluctantly we would have to do it for a year or two." Along with three other couples, they started the crisis pregnancy center.

"There were tens of thousands of students at Texas A&M, half of them women," Dr. Bradley said. "We asked the question, 'Are there women getting pregnant who don't want to be?' The answer is, of course there are. But we knew of no resource available that could help women in this situation to make the right decision and then to provide support all the way through. Not just when the baby is born but afterward with baby equipment, new parent counseling, adoption services, and so forth."

It was a bare-bones operation at the beginning. Ann and one of her friends were the counselors. They had no building, only a phone number, so they met young women in coffee shops and fast-food restaurants. "Now that we know what is involved, that is very stupid and naïve," Walter admitted, "but finally we worked all these things out."

The Brazos Valley Crisis Pregnancy Center was officially launched in 1985. Initially their small office was in Bryan, Texas (contiguous with College Station), several blocks down 29th Street from the eventual site of a Planned Parenthood Center, the one portrayed in the movie *Unplanned*. The sidewalk counselors would encourage ladies not to have an abortion but to go to the Brazos Valley Crisis Pregnancy center for help.

The pro-life movie *Unplanned* is the true story of the first closing of a Planned Parenthood Center (PPC) in the USA in Bryan, Texas, the result of a partnership between the sidewalk counselors stationed at PPC and the Brazos Valley Crisis Pregnancy Center Ann and Walter helped start.

Looking back, Walter and Ann wryly said they called it the Brazos Valley Financial Crisis Pregnancy Center because they had a financial crisis every month. For several years the organization ran on a shoestring. "At that time," Walter recalled, "the Catholic Church was much more tuned in on the issue of abortion." Protestant churches seemed not to encourage abortion, "but they weren't particularly against it either. I think they bought into the idea that an abortion is like an appendectomy."

Walter strongly disagreed with such a notion. "That's not the case," he said emphatically, "not when you see the unborn baby. There's a real baby in there, a human being. I saw a movie called *Silent Scream* that made me feel it was absolutely horrific that this practice had become so commonplace in our country. We needed to be doing everything we lawfully could to stem that tide."

As much as Walter wanted to be closely involved, he was already committed to other Christian work, and in time, the center became self-supporting. "I'm glad I didn't know it was going to take eight years to get up and running, but that's what it took," he said. "We felt like we couldn't stay involved long term because we were already called to the work we were doing on campus and also investing in it financially. Eventually we got enough people and financial resources that we were able to work our way out of it. After eight years we turned it over to a much bigger group

The Hope Pregnancy Center of Brazos Valley today. Their web site is HopePregnancy .org.

of friends who felt like that was the long-term call that God had on their lives.

"We were happy to plant the seeds and water them, then move back to the main things we felt called to do."

Like other seeds the Bradleys planted, the Crisis Pregnancy Center has grown strong in the years since, multiplying their faithful work on a scale they scarcely could have imagined. Now known as Hope Pregnancy Center of Brazos Valley, the center has a first-rate facility in College Station. Since 2006 they have offered ultrasounds to pregnant women along with a range of counseling services, all at no cost. They see more than 1,500 women a year as well as hundreds of their male partners, all with the mission "to honor God while meeting the needs of those facing crisis pregnancies." Some of their clients are students from countries where Christianity is suppressed or forbidden. Those people hear the gospel message for the first time in their lives from clinic staff and volunteers.

The center's expansion in recent years argues in favor of a divine hand at work. In 1999, Planned Parenthood opened their abortion clinic in Bryan. In 2013, Texas passed a law requiring abortion clinics to upgrade their medical facilities and staff them with doctors who had admitting privileges at local hospitals. In response, Planned Parenthood closed several of their clinics in the state, including the one in Bryan featured in the movie *Unplanned*. The next year the empty building was purchased from Planned Parenthood and reopened as a second pro-life resource focused on testing for sexually transmitted diseases. This new site expanded the center's reach from women who were possibly or already pregnant to those concerned about any of the health consequences of sexual activity. With characteristic understatement, Walter called the history of the center "pretty phenomenal. To think many of the women coming for help will save their baby's life, that's a pretty big thing to happen."

Even as a busy, ambitious, and successful engineering professor during his first years at Texas A&M, Walter Bradley lavished hundreds of hours a year on campus ministries and hundreds more on the pregnancy center. Yet during the same period he somehow found time to lead a team of authors in writing a book that carried his Christian principles to a far wider audience as it tackled the nexus of fascinating, contentious questions that boil to the surface where faith and science meet.

CHAPTER 6

The Intersection of Faith and Science

One of the most significant and far-reaching projects of Walter Bradley's career had a long gestation period. *The Mystery of Life's Origin* grew from the seeds of a friendship planted in the 1960s. This book brought together Dr. Bradley's views on science and faith, his skilled presentation of scientific facts, his clarity of thought and organization of details as a teacher, and his unique brand of cordial relentlessness in advancing the view that life on earth could not have originated by natural, random means alone.

Because the book combines so many of Bradley's interests and facets of his work, and because it forms the basis for his popular scientific presentation on how our world came to be—a presentation that has been given more than a hundred times over the years to tens of thousands of people and is still being given today—this book and its case for the origin of life are worthy of a closer look.

The stage for writing *The Mystery of Life's Origin* was set while Walter was working on his PhD at the University of Texas and met Jon Buell, the campus director of Campus Crusade for Christ. Walter was getting more involved in campus ministry through CCC at the time, and the two developed a friendship. As we noted in chapter 4, a few years later, in 1972, Buell and his colleague Jimmy Williams started Probe Ministries in Dallas to set up speaking opportunities for visiting Christian professors

Two covers for *The Mystery of Life's Origin*.

on secular college campuses. These programs, Walter realized, "got me interested in using my own background in science to explore questions at the interface of faith and science for my own benefit and to be able to address these questions for others."

At the intersection of faith and science, those who study the origins of life generally take one of two paths. One group believes life on earth is the product of chemical evolution (as distinct from biological evolution) and that the first living organisms developed somehow on their own from nonliving organic matter. Over billions of years, chance and the laws of nature eventually made up for the long odds against spontaneous evolution and produced the spark of life. The other camp believes that non-living organic matter cannot become living organisms without supernatural intervention, because no mechanism exists in the natural world that can produce such a change, no matter how much time is available.

Scientists tend to support one position or the other based on their preconceived notions about God as the Creator. If they believe the universe formed on its own according to natural laws, they accept chemical evolution alone as a sufficient explanation for the origin of life. If they believe God made the universe—that its origin is outside of nature (i.e., "supernatural")—they reject a purely naturalistic explanation for the origin of life. While it is possible that God could have made a universe with the intrinsic potential to have the first living system unfold on its own, the evidence for such a presupposition is lacking based on what we know today. As a scientist and a Christian, Dr. Bradley believes that the laws of nature are God's customary way of creating and caring for His creation and that miracles are God creating and caring for His creation in some extraordinary way. Many modern scientists would agree with famous scientists from the past, such as Pascal, Newton, Maxwell, and Boyle, that the more we observe and learn about the universe, and especially about living systems, the more we see the "fingerprints" of God everywhere. Life does not appear to be the result of random chemical processes but rather the ordered work of an intelligent maker.

In 1976, Dr. Bradley agreed to Jon Buell's offer to explore the status of origin of life research to evaluate what it implied. Two coauthors eventually joined in the effort. Dr. Charles Thaxton, who became part of the Probe ministries staff around 1978 and held a PhD in biochemistry, added his expertise to the project. Later, when they needed a chapter in geochemistry, Bradley and Thaxton invited Dr. Roger Olsen to bring his knowledge of that field into the mix.

Dr. Bradley's background in polymer science, thermodynamic, and chemical kinetic was ideal for this project. Thaxton's and Olsen's backgrounds were perfect compliments to Bradley's, and together they covered all the important bases.

Walter found significant fundamental issues in these theories of the origin of life, the discussion of which made for an excellent presentation. By the time Buell and Williams started their Collegiate Speaker program in Probe Ministries, Walter was ready to give talks on thermodynamics and the origin of life. His first opportunity came as part of a Probe Collegiate Speak program at Colorado State University. As he recalled, "I was pleased to discover, talking to a class of a hundred seniors who were biochemistry majors and five professors of biochemistry at Colorado State, that the questions I was raising regarding the thermodynamic challenges to the origin of life were conceded to be real by the professors of these classes who never had these problems brought to their attention—partly because their background in biochemistry was much stronger than in physical chemistry."

Dr. Bradley's previous experience speaking on the subject gave him valuable insights as the book manuscript took shape. As he explained in a recent interview, questions and comments from audience members helped refine the narrative. "If I made claims that were wrong or stupid, people were happy to bring them to my attention. Before we wrote *The Mystery of Life's Origin* we got lots of feedback from Q&As after public presentations, which helped make it better." Walter also attended a Gordon Research conference on the origin of life while he and his co-authors were writing the book. The conference, he said, "provided wonderful opportunities to hear cutting-edge talks on the origin of life from leading researchers in the field as well as opportunities to visit with them personally."

Bradley credits Buell's "very diligent work" in securing Philosophical Library as the publisher for the book, which was titled in full *The*

Mystery of Life's Origin: Reassessing Current Theories. Buell approached twenty-seven secular publishers before Philosophical Library agreed to publish it. Walter commented, "He was wise to be persistent because it would not have been read, much less taken seriously, by secular scientists had we used a Christian publisher." Buell also found three outstanding researchers in the origin-of-life field to read the work who subsequently gave excellent jacket endorsements. Consequently, the book was reviewed in top journals, including *Chemical and Engineering News*, the most widely read journal by chemist and chemical engineers.

It is worth noting that the three co-authors decided to discuss the religious and philosophical implications of *Mystery* only in an epilogue. Separating the scientific discussion from the philosophical implications was instrumental in it being widely read in the origin-of-life research community.

First released in 1984, *Mystery* became, in Walter's words, "the launching pad for a path to many wonderful opportunities to speak on faith and science for the next thirty-five years." The book received numerous glowing reviews. Robert Jastrow, founder of the Goddard Institute for Space Studies of NASA, called it a "valuable summary of the evidence against chemical evolution of life out of non-living matter." Dr. Robert Shapiro of New York University and co-author of *Life Beyond Earth* wrote, "The authors have made an important contribution to the origin of life field." To biology professor Dean Kenyon of San Francisco State, the book's "arguments are cogent, original and compelling. . . . The authors believe, and now I concur, that there is a fundamental flaw in all current theories of the chemical origins of life."

"This is really a brilliant book," wrote chemist and origin-of-life researcher Clifford Matthews at the University of Illinois. "A superb re-evaluation, it's very fair and it's not a polemic." Matthews liked *Mystery* so much that he called the authors to order ten copies for his graduate students to read.

More open praise rolled in from scientists in relevant fields. Molecular biologist Jay Roth at the University of Connecticut was "greatly impressed" and called *Mystery* a "fascinating scholarly work." Chemist Walter Thorson at the University of Alberta praised it as a "splendid book" offering

Ann and Walter Bradley in 1982.

"very careful and scientific argumentation." Physicist Graham Gutsche at the US Naval Academy said it was "Outstanding!" and noted that he "used the information in my teaching."

Chemical & Engineering News gave the job of reviewing it to chemist Richard Lemmon at the Lawrence Berkeley National Laboratory. His review in the July 1, 1985, issue began, "The only people to whom I can recommend *The Mystery of Life's Origin: Reassessing Current Theories* are the minuscule fraction of C&EN's readers who are religious creationists. These also are people who are prone to write letters to the editor whenever anything touching on creationism appears. I look forward to the forthcoming complaints about this review."

Eugene C. McKannan at NASA's Marshall Space Flight Center calculated that "57% of [Lemmon's] review is about the reviewer's beliefs—not about the book" and skewered Lemmon's "circular logic."

Lemmon's UC Berkeley colleague Henry F. Schaefer III said Lemmon's was a "superficial review." Schaefer read their book and found it to be both interesting and provocative." He noted that the authors "are

When Lemmon gives your book a sour review, make
Lemmonade.

not 'creationists' in the sense popularized by recent court cases." Schaefer
has since gone on to fame as one of the most highly cited chemists in the
world.

In *Mystery*, Walter and his collaborators argue that it is impossible to
prove the existence of God using the tools of science, since science can
only explore physical phenomena. Nevertheless, the nature of nature—
the comprehensibility of nature through the eyes of science—points to
the highly likely existence of an intelligent creator. The fine-tuning of the
laws of nature and the universal constants (a mystery in their own right)
provide a suitable habitat for carbon-based life. In *The Mystery of Life's
Origin*, Walter and his co-authors set out not to prove the existence of a
supernatural creator but to test the hypothesis that without one, according
to the laws of the universe none of us would be here.

The authors carefully explore and document the overwhelming obstacles that must be overcome to go from simple building blocks that could have been available on a prebiotic earth to the complex polymers, DNA, RNA, and other ingredients necessary for life. Thirty-five years after the book's publication, these same biochemical problems persist. The study of the origin of life today certainly favors the possibility, maybe even the likelihood, that an intelligent creator was involved.

In their book Walter and his colleagues wrote, "We know that in numerous cases certain effects always have intelligent causes, such as dictionaries, sculptures, machines and paintings. We reason by analogy that similar effects also have intelligent causes. For example, after looking up to see 'BUY FORD' spelled out in smoke across the sky we infer the presence of a skywriter even if we heard or saw no airplane. We would similarly conclude the presence of intelligent activity were we to come upon an elephant-shaped mud image in a cedar forest. . . .

"Why then doesn't the message sequence on the DNA molecule also constitute *prima facie* evidence for an intelligent source? After all, DNA information is not just analogous to a message sequence such as Morse code, it *is* such a message sequence. . . . We believe that if this question is considered, it will be seen that most often it is answered in the negative simply because it is thought to be inappropriate to bring a Creator into science."

The ability to reproduce by replicating DNA is one of the most basic characteristics of life. There is no known way for nonliving organic matter that lacks DNA to acquire it by natural evolutionary means. In a nutshell, Dr. Bradley and his co-authors hypothesized that nonliving, or abiotic, material (mud, protein, amino acids) cannot transform itself into even the simplest living organism (virus, bacteria, yeast). No amount or form of energy (lightning, earthquakes, radiation) over any number of years (even back to the Big Bang 14 billion years ago) can turn any body of abiotic organic chemicals (tidal pools, organic soup, chemical clouds) into a living thing.

This is due to observable laws and relationships that define and control the known universe. Bradley explains the importance of the laws of thermodynamics in considering whether or not life could have formed on its own. "The First Law of Thermodynamics states that the total energy of the universe or any isolated part of it will be the same after any transformation of matter and energy as it was before," he begins. "This is also known as the Principle of the Conservation of Energy. Change in energy equals the work done plus heat.

"The Second Law of Thermodynamics describes the flow of energy in nature in processes which are irreversible. Energy always flows toward a more uniform distribution of energy in the universe. Gasoline is an energy-rich compound; burning it produces mechanical work plus energy-lean compounds of carbon dioxide and water. The flow of energy divided by temperature is the entropy. If you turn off the heat, the temperatures equalize and the rate of change of entropy goes to zero. Energy flows in the direction that causes total energy to be more uniformly distributed. The Second Law of Thermodynamics indicates that the entropy of the universe is always increasing; energy is becoming more uniformly distributed."

The authors then explain how thermodynamics argue against the theory of evolution. "Since the important macromolecules of living systems (DNA, protein, etc.) are more energy rich than their precursors (amino acids, heterocyclic bases, phosphates, and sugars), classical thermodynamics would predict that such macromolecules will not spontaneously form." Energy flowing through a solution containing simple chemical building blocks can in principle be driven up the hill energetically to more complex molecular structures, but it requires more complex energy-processing chemical systems.

The authors continue, "The probability of the formation of one bacterium from simple precursors within five billion years is one in 10^{11} [one followed by eleven zeros]. The probability that at ordinary temperature a macroscopic number of molecules is assembled to give rise to the highly ordered structures and to the coordinated functions characterizing living organisms is vanishingly small. The idea of spontaneous genesis of life in its present form is therefore highly improbable, even on the scale of billions of years during which prebiotic chemical evolution occurred."

The essential point here is that energy does not necessarily produce structure. "The work necessary to polymerize DNA and protein molecules from simple biomonomers could *potentially* be accomplished by energy flow through the system," the authors explain. "Still, we know that such energy flow is a necessary but not sufficient condition for polymerization of the macromolecules of life. Arranging a pile of bricks into the configuration of a house requires work. One would hardly expect to accomplish this work with dynamite, however. Not only must energy flow through the system, it must be coupled in some specific way to the work to be done. . . . The coupling of energy flow to the specific work requirements in the formation of DNA and protein is particularly important since the required configurational entropy work of coding is substantial."

Before researchers realized that living systems were so complex, many people thought that, given enough time, life would originate by sheer chance. In the 1860s, Pasteur performed experiments to demonstrate that spontaneous genesis does not occur. Many experiments from 1951 to the present have tried unsuccessfully to discover a biochemical pathway to life. The role of chance in the origin of life has been strongly challenged. Chance reactions and reconfigurations can change the structure of matter but cannot add new information to it. They cannot bring nonliving material to life.

Bradley adds that the importance of complexity over order "has come from the observation that the essential ingredients for replicating a system—enzymes and nucleic acids—are all information-bearing molecules. In contrast consider crystals. They are very orderly, spatially periodic arrangements of atoms (or molecules) but they carry very little information—analogous to a book with only one sentence repeated over and over: highly ordered but little information."

Bradley continues, "There is a general relationship between information and entropy [the general trend of the universe toward disorder and randomness]. . . . The information content in a given sequence of units, be they digits in a number, letters in a sentence, or amino acids in a polypeptide or protein, depends on the minimum number of instructions needed to specify or describe the structure. Only a few instructions are needed to define an ordered structure such as a crystal. A couple of sentences will do. Many instructions are needed to specify DNA. To synthesize the DNA of an *E. coli* bacterium would take about 4 million instructions."

For decades, scientists have conducted experiments to demonstrate that life can emerge from nonliving material. Without exception, contemporary experiments fail to prove the hypothesis that life developed unassisted from nonliving forms. Bradley and his co-authors underscore the point: "We know by experience that intelligent investigators can synthesize proteins and build genes. [Yet] we still have no evidence it can be done by unassisted abiotic means. The earliest organisms appear suddenly without any evidence of a pre-biotic soup or simpler precursors."

Bradley continues, "So-called protocells have been produced in the laboratory in an attempt to bridge the nonliving and the living. Such structures do have the crude resemblance to true cells but none of the internal cellular machinery, such as enzymes, DNA, or phospholipid cell membranes. The few 'cell' functions manifested by protocell systems typically arise from simple physical forces. Any similarity to true cellular processes is highly superficial."

One difficulty in staging a credible experiment is that there are no set standards for what constitutes interference in what should be a natural process. The authors write, "The usual interpretation of chemical evolution derives a great deal of apparent plausibility from reports of laboratory prebiotic simulation experiments. In fact most of these experiments are probably invalid. Unlike other established experimental disciplines, 'prebiotic chemistry' has no generally accepted criterion for what constitutes a valid prebiotic simulation experiment. Consequently, many incredible experiments have been published as 'simulation' experiments. . . .

"When it is acknowledged that most so-called probiotic simulation experiments actually owe their success to the crucial but *illegitimate* role of the investigator, a new and fresh phase of the experimental approach to life's origin can then be entered. Until then however, the literature of chemical evolution will probably continue to be dominated by reports of experiments in which the investigator . . . will have performed work on the system through intelligent, exogenous intervention. Such work establishes experimental boundary conditions, and imposes intelligent influence/control over a supposedly 'prebiotic' earth. As long as this informative interference of the investigator is ignored, the illusion of prebiotic simulation will be fostered. We would predict that this practice will prove to be a barrier to solving the mystery of life's origin."

Dr. Bradley points out, "Leading researchers in the field agree that the truth about how life began remains a mystery."

He continues, "Many facts have come to light in the past three decades of experimental inquiry into life's beginning. With each passing year the criticism has gotten stronger. The advance of science itself is what is challenging the notion that life arose on earth by spontaneous (in a thermo-dynamic sense) chemical reactions."

One dramatic illustration in *The Mystery of Life's Origin* of the degree of precision required for life to form is to look at conditions surrounding the Big Bang, the great explosion that gave birth to the universe. The Big Bang followed the physics of any explosion, though on an inconceivably large scale. The authors note, "The critical boundary condition for the Big Bang is its initial velocity. If this velocity is too fast, the matter in the universe expands too quickly and never coalesces into planets, stars, and galaxies. If the initial velocity is too slow, the universe expands only for a short time and then quickly collapses under the influence of gravity. Well-accepted cosmological models tell us that the initial velocity must be specified to a precision of 10^{-60} [a decimal point followed by 59 zeros and a one, about the same chance as flipping a coin 200 times and it coming up heads every time]. This requirement seems to overwhelm chance." As we will soon see, other variables that are essential for life on earth overwhelm chance in similar fashion, to the point where, between the beginning of the universe and the present day, the number of "chances" for success has been exhausted, limited by the number of molecules in creation.

Dr. Bradley points out that the study of chemical evolution is like forensic science, which is based on interpreting evidence that can be duplicated in the lab. Investigators report circumstantial evidence for the naturalistic origin of life based on assumptions that conditions on the early earth were different from today but that chemical processes were the same. According to this uniformitarian thinking, if scientists can accurately re-create the conditions of pre-biotic earth, then they should be able to reproduce the process that led to the earliest life forms under those conditions.

The modern theory of chemical evolution "envisions that the atmosphere of the early earth contained such gases as hydrogen, methane, carbon monoxide, carbon dioxide, ammonia, and nitrogen, but no free oxygen. While this atmosphere would be quite toxic to us, its reducing quality was hospitable to organic molecules. Some time close to 3.5 billion years ago, the earth cooled to under 100 degrees centigrade. This allowed for the survival of organic molecules that would have degraded at higher temperatures. Various forms of energy drove reactions in the atmosphere and ocean to form a wide variety of simple organic molecules—ultraviolet rays, lightning, geothermal heat, atmospheric shock waves from thunder.

"Simple compounds formed in the atmosphere were washed by rain into the oceans. Here they gathered with accumulating organic matter, producing a 'hot dilute soup.' Flooding and evaporation concentrated the chemicals. Clays in the basins had a catalytic effect on the process. Gradually these compounds produced protocells, eventually developing nucleic acids that were further refined into living cells."

But how scientifically plausible is this previously widely accepted version of the origin of life? Would primordial chemical compounds actually react in that way? How can we know? Bradley and his team examine some of the problems with accurately simulating chemical evolution. They counter that "early energy would be more likely to destroy compounds than to form them. Atmospheric ammonia would have been degraded in as little as ten years. Hydrogen sulfide would have been photolyzed into free sulfur and hydrogen in no more than 10,000 years. Amino acid concentrations were likely one in 10^{-12} [a decimal followed by eleven zeroes and a one], far too dilute for the spontaneous formation of proteins. This is based on the rate of formation of amino acids compared with their decomposition by ultraviolet rays in the atmosphere."

In summary, Dr. Bradley writes, "If there ever was a prebiotic oceanic soup of chemicals, it would have been too dilute for chemical evolution rates to have been significant. . . . Both in the atmosphere and in the various water basins of the primitive earth, many destructive interactions would have so vastly diminished, if not altogether consumed, essential precursor chemicals, that chemical evolution rates would have been negligible. The soup would have been too dilute for direct polymerization to occur. Even local ponds for concentrating soup ingredients would have met with the same problem. Furthermore, no geological evidence indicates an organic soup, even a small organic pond, ever existed on this planet."

Chemical evolution fails to explain the jump from organic chemicals simple enough to have formed in a tidal pool to the vastly more complex forms of even the most basic living organisms. As Dr. Bradley and his co-authors write, "The enigma of the origin of life comes in the difficulty of imagining a biological system that is sufficiently complex to process energy, store information, and replicate, and yet at the same time is sufficiently simple to have just 'happened' in a warm pond, as Darwin suggested, or elsewhere."

In his popular presentation on the origins of life, Dr. Bradley invites his audience to step back and consider the minimal needs to be satisfied for a universe to be capable of supporting life of any imaginable type, and how those needs are all interconnected. To illustrate, he imagines dropping a water balloon from the Leaning Tower of Pisa onto a friend walking below. To hit his target, he has to know the strength of the gravity force constant, the height of the release point, and the mathematical formula that describes the relationship of the velocity of the falling balloon to the gravitational attraction between the earth and the balloon as a function of time, in order to calculate when to release the balloon. Certain conditions (gravity) are constant while others (time of release) are not. But all conditions have to mesh perfectly for Bradley's friend to get soaked.

He also compares origin of creation theories to reverse engineering a car, starting with the finished vehicle and working backward to the original design. Every detail of the car is defined by physical laws so that a change in one component causes a ripple effect of changes in everything else. The least miscalculation and the car won't run at all. The automotive engineer has no control over laws of nature, mathematical formulas, or universal constants such as the force of gravity. And even components he can control (size, weight, passenger capacity) are interrelated and therefore cannot be independently specified or assigned. The greater this interdependence of specified boundary conditions ("the car must hold four passengers and get thirty miles per gallon"), the more complex and demanding the design process. Bradley notes, "Small errors in the specification of any requirement will produce either a car with very poor performance or, worse, a car that does not function at all." This interdependence is multiplied to a degree beyond imagining when designing even the simplest living organisms.

Dr. Bradley uses another entertaining example to explain to his audiences the need for some intervening force to shape and control the creative process. "If I stand across the street and throw paint at my curb, I am not very likely to paint '204,' which is my house number. On the other hand, if I first place a template with the numbers '204' on my curb and then sling paint, I can easily paint '204' on my curb. Living systems contain their own templates. However, such templates did not guide the process before life began (i.e., under prebiotic conditions). How, then, did the templates and other molecular machinery develop?" If no intelligent maker cut the house number stencil, where did it come from?

Dr. Bradley and his co-authors assert that life is too complex to have formed at random, even over billions of years. "To illustrate the staggering degree of complexity involved here," the authors write, "let us consider a typical protein that is composed of 100 amino acids. Amino acids are molecules that can have two mirror image structures, usually referred to as 'left-handed' and 'right-handed' variants. A functional protein requires the amino acids from which it is built to be (1) all left-handed; (2) all linked together with peptide bonds; and (3) all in just the right sequence to fold up into the three-dimensional structure needed for biological function. The probability of correctly assembling a functional protein in one try in a prebiotic pond is 10^{-190} [the same as the chance of flipping a coin 631 times and it coming up heads every time]. If we took all the carbon in the universe, converted it into amino acids, and allowed it to chemically react at the maximum permissible rate of 10^{13} interactions per second for five billion years, the probability of making a single functioning protein increases to only 10^{-60}. For this reason, chance explanations for the origin of life have been rejected. Some non-random process or intelligent designer must be responsible. However, there are no apparent non-random processes (such as natural selection is claimed to be in evolution) that would seem capable of generating the required complexity and information for the first living system.

"Making a viable protein from scratch is analogous to writing a sentence in a language with 20 letters in the alphabet (e.g., amino acids), using a random sequencing of the letters as well as random orientations (that is upside down or sideways). Creating a coherent sentence or short paragraph from such a random sequencing of letters strains the imagination. Creating a functioning living system becomes as arduous as writing a long paragraph with such an inefficient approach. These information-generating requirements present the single, greatest obstacle to a purely naturalistic explanation for the origin of life."

Bradley makes a compelling case that with all the time in the world—literally—random reactions would not have produced life. Moreover, according to the laws of thermodynamics, creation on its own would have always tended to become less organized, not more, without a local organizing force or process in nature.

In *The Mystery of Life's Origin*, the writers note that today computers can simulate billions of years of chemical processes based on the model of neo-Darwinian evolution. The results show that life could not have originated by chance within 10 billion years—twice the age of the earth. While evolutionists insist that the issue here is faulty programming, the results illustrate the ongoing problem with probability calculations. As Dr. Bradley and his co-authors note, "Such calculations must first assume a plausible chemical pathway, or course of events, and then calculate the probability of this series of events, in the hope that the answer will at least approximate the probability of the *actual* course of events. Nevertheless, there is great uncertainly about the actual chemical pathway."

These traditional probability calculations have now been superseded by others that do not require exact details of the events leading to the first life on earth. The authors write that recent advances in the application of the first and second laws of thermodynamics to living systems provide the basis for these newer calculations, adding, "Through them, accurate probabilities for the spontaneous synthesis of complex chemicals can be calculated without regard to the path that led to their development."

Those calculations, Dr. Bradley and his colleagues conclude, prove that "reasonable doubt exists concerning whether simple chemicals on a primitive earth did spontaneously evolve (or organize themselves) into the first life. We leave it to the jury to decide."

His views on the origins of life and fine-tuning of the universe have given Dr. Bradley a platform with audiences across the country to question the assumption of methodological naturalism, which assumes that in scientific research all processes in nature over the entire natural history must be assumed to be natural (i.e., no miracles). All observations must ultimately be found to have a natural explanation. The authors of *Mystery* would agree that most observed effects do have a natural cause. But to assume that all current observations and historical ones must be found to have a natural explanation is presumptuous.

Some observations like the fine-tuning of the universe and the origin of life seem to defy naturalistic explanation. As Dr. Bradley explained in an interview, "While they may be found to have naturalistic explanation in the future, inference to the best explanation today is to accept the possibility that an intelligent creator may be the best explanation, based on what we know today. It is the nature of what we observe but cannot explain that points to an intelligent creator, not just the absence of a natural explanation." What we discover in the future should tell us more about *how* God executed His creative work.

Dr. Bradley has had the opportunity to speak on seventy-seven university campuses, making about 140 presentations to more than fifty thousand students and professors over the past thirty-five years. His faith and his scientific evidence grow stronger with every encounter. As he said recently, "I must conclude that it takes a great deal more faith to believe in an accidental universe than to believe in an intelligent creator, or God, who crafted such a marvelous universe and beautiful place of habitation in planet Earth, and then created life—including human beings—to occupy it."

When Dr. Bradley gave his talk on the origin of life at the University of California, Berkeley, several years after the book came out, 1,800 people attended. He considered speeches like that one "low-hanging fruit," and regularly scheduled talks on faith and science around his travel to material science conferences to present his work in polymeric composite materials, though he also took time occasionally to make a specific trip for a presentation on how life came to be.

Over thirty-five years later, Charles Thaxton, Walter Bradley, and Roger Olsen are joined by their wives to celebrate the launch of the reissued and updated version of *The Mystery of Life's Origin* at Discovery Institute's January 2020 Dallas Conference on Science and Faith.

The public debate about faith and science also brought Dr. Bradley and me (Dembski) together, initiating a friendship that has grown stronger in the years since. We both consider the other to be a key player in the field of intelligent design, the idea that life on earth had to be the product of an intelligent designer, whether God or some other supernatural entity.

In the twenty-first century there is a large and growing body of research and commentary on the concept of intelligent design (ID), of which I have been considered a frontline proponent and apologist. But when Bradley's book was published in 1984, it was one of the earliest detailed analyses and explanations of the ID concept. Around that time, I publicly identified Bradley as "the father of Intelligent Design."

"There's probably some truth to that," Bradley modestly acknowledged, but added that "Dembski, Michael Behe, Steve Meyer, and others planted many new seeds of their own. I planted seeds in the origin of life garden and they planted in the evolution of life garden. These people have essentially invested their careers in addressing faith and science and have ultimately been able to do much more than I have because it was their primary focus. And they are really smart guys!"

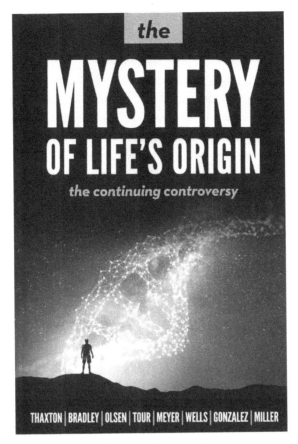

2020 edition from Discovery Institute Press

"In many cases some of the insights I eventually used beyond what I'd developed for myself were insights that had been discovered by Bill Dembski, Steve Meyer, and other of his contemporaries at the Discovery Institute. I have been very blessed and benefited by a lot of the work they did. We had some of the early pioneering ideas that we were kicking around and developing, and because these others came along, and because they're very smart and put in a lot of time and effort, they were able to shape those arguments and enlarge them. In that way we've been collaborators. I was probably a little bit earlier than some of these guys, but the contributions they made are in my opinion much more significant.

"I'll acknowledge what Bill [Dembski] said, that I was maybe one who co-authored one of the first books that kind of kicked things off, but I will also say that the people who came after me did a whole lot more. I should also acknowledge the role that the Discovery Institute has played in providing both a 'think tank' for ongoing collaborative research and multiple means for propagating these ideas through websites, videos, technical monographs, and conferences."

Mystery continues to foster discussion and debate. It's been more than thirty-five years since its release. Has the original analysis by Thaxton, Bradley, and Olsen survived advances in science? A 2020 update titled *The Mystery of Life's Origin: The Continuing Controversy* says yes. Published by Discovery Institute Press, this refreshed and enlarged edition includes a section called "The State of the Debate," as well as new confirming chapters by noted synthetic biochemist James Tour, physicist Brian Miller, astronomer Guillermo Gonzalez, biologist Jonathan Wells, and philosopher of science Stephen Meyer.

The origin of life from a materialistic cause remains as much a mystery as it did thirty-five years before.

CHAPTER 7

Polymers, Pizza, and Parenting

Walter Bradley's interest in intelligent design, keen though it was, never distracted him from his professional work. Experience reinforced the lesson that as a man of faith, the time he spent with family, at church, and being involved in Christian ministries meant less time available for pursuing research funding, conducting research, and writing journal articles. But it was important not to let his faith sidetrack him or be an excuse for substandard performance. Publicly identified as a Christian, Bradley held himself to the highest standards because he knew others were watching and judging him every day, wondering, how will "the Christian professor" handle this challenge or that situation? Bradley continued his long list of activities and responsibilities in stride along three parallel tracks: Dr. Bradley the prolific professor and scientist; Walter the tireless Christian friend, host, and Bible teacher; and the father and family man.

Bradley's academic environment was far bigger and more diverse now than it had been at Colorado School of Mines. There Bradley had been one of 160 professors. At Texas A&M University he joined a faculty of 2,300 professors. The move to TAMU also gave Dr. Bradley expanded opportunities in his new field of concentration: the high-performance polymers and polymeric composite materials that were replacing metals in some automotive and aerospace industries components. Because Texas is the worldwide center of polypropylene and polyethylene (polyolefin) production and research, with three-quarters of the nation's polyolefin production capacity within fifty miles of Houston, A&M was ideally positioned to develop world-class polymer programs that benefited petrochemical companies, manufacturers, and the state of Texas.

Dr. Bradley soon made his professional mark on the A&M campus. In 1978, he received the annual award for best materials paper from the American Nuclear Society for his work in liquid lithium corrosion of steel, the paper he had co-authored while still at Colorado School of Mines. For the 1980–81 academic year, he was awarded the Halliburton Professorship for the College of Engineering, a rotating professorship endowed by Halliburton, a worldwide oilfield services company headquartered in Houston. Both the American Nuclear Society and Halliburton honors reflected Dr. Bradley's interest in applying scientific engineering knowledge to practical applications that benefit businesses and communities.

Another appointment further underscored Dr. Bradley's interest in converting scientific knowledge into practical benefits. In 1982, Bradley was selected as a Research Fellow in the Texas A&M Engineering Experiment Station, which is a state of Texas Engineering Research Agency. TEES forms partnerships with industry, academia, and community groups to benefit economic development, education, health, and the environment. In 1985, Bradley was named a Senior Research Fellow at TAMU in recognition of the impact of his outstanding research, a position he held as long as he was on the faculty at Texas A&M.

Four years later he was appointed head of the Department of Mechanical Engineering and its sixty-seven faculty members. It was— and remains—the largest mechanical engineering department in the country and rose to be ranked twelfth out of three hundred mechanical engineering departments in the United States at the end of Dr. Bradley's four-year term. (Today it is ranked seventh.) Twice before he accepted this appointment, Walter declined offers by his department colleagues and the dean to be a candidate for the job. Dr. Bradley's externally funded research programs were doing extremely well, and he still had high school age children at home. However, by 1989, the mechanical engineering department was struggling from financial mismanagement and the perception that some professors were getting preferential resources at the expense of others. With his two children now attending the University of Texas and the need to create a new atmosphere of fairness in the department, Walter agreed to be a candidate.

With overwhelming support from Dr. Bradley's colleagues, the dean appointed him the new head of mechanical engineering. In his final interview with the dean and four associate deans, the last question they asked was whether his Christian beliefs would create any issues in his performance as department head. He immediately answered yes. After a long, pregnant pause, he said it would cause him to treat everyone in the department with respect, to allocate travel funds and other resources fairly, and to work hard to help each professor realize his or her full potential. Dr. Bradley had already distributed a detailed five-page outline of the changes he would make if appointed. While many of his colleagues were not people of faith, they still appreciated Dr. Bradley's high ethical standards and felt they could trust him.

Dr. Bradley's seemingly endless energy and enthusiasm coupled with his natural gift for leadership made him well-suited for the headship position. Fortunately for Walter, TAMU department heads had a great deal of autonomy. "Some universities have department chairs who function with the same limitations as a committee chair," he later explained, "namely, everything gets done by majority vote." A&M department chairs, on the other hand, "have the authority to do whatever they please, including ignore the majority of the faculty." Though warned not to overspend his $5 million annual budget, Dr. Bradley could use it as he saw fit. "I was not micromanaged by the dean or subject to majority rule of the faculty." This was a good thing, Walter believed. "Some changes that needed to be made were not necessarily changes that a simple majority of the professors would favor, but the changes were necessary to move the department forward."

Dr. Bradley began implementing the changes he promised right away. His first year as department head he combined all of the budgeted funds for travel, graders, photocopies, and long-distance phone calls from the previous year into one account that was divided evenly between the sixty-seven professors. This resolved the problem of perceived unfairness in these areas and also motivated professors to spend their money more carefully. For example, if they traveled more economically to conferences, they had more funds for graders or even additional trips. "We got a big boost in morale and a great deal more benefit from this departmental resource," Dr. Bradley said.

His first year as head, Dr. Bradley also adjusted classroom teaching loads based on each professor's involvement in research. It was not fair for a professor with no externally funded projects and no graduate students to teach the same number of classes as a professor supervising eight PhD students supported by external research funding. Those more involved in research should have reduced teaching loads. Those who favored teaching over research should teach more. By enabling the faculty not active in research to teach more, the teaching load of active researchers was reduced thereby enhancing the overall departmental research effort. Dr. Bradley never had one complaint about this change.

Dr. Bradley conducted his first-year annual reviews with careful diligence, collecting individual data on teaching, graduate student supervision, research funding, technical publications, and service to the department, then explaining to each professor how they were doing relative to other department faculty. Bradley concluded each review with suggestions on how they could improve their performance and provided or suggested resources that could help them.

As he helped department faculty, Dr. Bradley also wanted to serve and help his staff of roughly twenty-five. Most of them were recent hires earning entry-level salaries independent of their background. Doing so was a false economic strategy employed by some previous department heads. When salary is not linked with experience, better staff will move to another department that pays better. Some senior staff in Dr. Bradley's department were unproductive and had bad attitudes. On his first day as department head, Dr. Bradley met with his staff to share his vision for the department and the key role the staff would need to play. He explained that anyone not willing to work hard with their heads and their hands would be terminated, but all who were willing to work hard could expect a 33 percent raise during Dr. Bradley's four-year term. Over that time the staff shrank by 25 percent through attrition or termination, he said, adding that the money saved went to salary increases for the remainder.

He also said he wanted each staff member to take one day a month for additional training to improve their skills and productivity. It was a highly productive and successful meeting. During Dr. Bradley's four years as department head there was not a single staff resignation. Ten were released and staff salaries were raised 33 percent as promised.

From the beginning, Dr. Bradley treated the staff to monthly luncheons to get feedback on how the department could operate more efficiently, serve students and professors better, and save money. Many of his best ideas came from staff members, who deeply appreciated being treated with respect and having their ideas solicited and considered. By the end of Dr. Bradley's term staff morale was sky high, a remarkable turnaround from before.

Relocating to such a large campus naturally brought Walter and Ann fresh opportunities to share their Christian worldview. As they had done in Colorado, they found many ways to bring people together to discuss ideas of life and faith. One of their favorites was what Walter called "pizza and a movie night." One Friday night a month he invited all of the students in his two classes to his home to eat pizza and then watch a movie that raised interesting questions about life, sparking robust discussions afterward. One of Dr. Bradley's favorite films for these get-togethers was *Crimes and Misdemeanors*. In this award-winning Woody Allen classic, a wealthy eye doctor is afraid his mistress is going to tell his wife of their affair. He allows his brother to arrange his mistress's murder, which is eventually blamed on an innocent drifter. The story raises thought-provoking questions about justice, morality, and God's place in the world: If there is no God, can there be a moral structure to the universe?

Another featured movie was *Out of Africa*, winner of the 1986 Best Picture Academy Award, which asks: Can there be loving relationships without commitment? Is there such a thing as free love, or is there a cost of commitment that must be paid? These movies were not explicitly religious but addressed religious matters implicitly. *Citizen Kane*, *Les Misérables*, and *Chariots of Fire* were some of the other movies Ann and Walter presented.

Typically twenty to thirty students would come over from 5:00 to 8:00 p.m., a schedule that allowed the Bradleys to avoid competing with Friday-night parties and athletic events.

Another form of Dr. Bradley's "pizza ministry" was to host a party the last day of the semester at the pizza parlor across from his office for any of his students interested in a free lunch and learning how and why he became a follower of Jesus. In addition to the fifteen or twenty students who typically attended, other people in the restaurant would often eavesdrop.

Bradley relishes memories of some of the students touched by these events. One of many who came for pizza and a movie was Paul, the best student in his class that spring semester, who began his faith journey at one of the pizza dinners with *Crimes and Misdemeanors* for "dessert." After defending his PhD dissertation six years later, Paul wrote Dr. Bradley a letter saying he wanted to be a Christian professor so he could be to his students what Bradley had been for him.

Dr. Bradley also made Christmas a time for sharing the Christian message. He bought quantities of Lee Strobel's book, *The Case for Christ*, and put them in a box outside his classrooms during fall semester final exams. Students were invited to take a copy as his Christmas gift to them. Amazingly, 50 to 60 percent of students would take a book. Dr. Bradley said, "I was blessed to hear back from some of them that reading the book had led them to a Christian profession of faith, or at least had put them on a spiritual journey."

Of course Walter and Ann eagerly extended the same signature hospitality to friends and colleagues. One strategy was for Walter to organize a lunchtime Bible study built around books he thought would appeal to his professional peers. One book was *How to Be a Christian Without Being Religious* by Fritz Ridenour. When one of the men invited said he wasn't very religious, Bradley replied that in that case this was the perfect book for him. This man came to the study and eventually became a committed Christian, conquering his alcoholism and generously volunteering his time to help other alcoholics.

The Bradleys also hosted regular four-week discussion-dessert series. Based on an approach developed by Search Ministries of Fort Worth, Texas, these were informal gatherings co-hosted by the Bradleys and four other Christian couples, each of whom invited five more couples. Twenty of the thirty attendees were non-Christians and they posed the discussion questions. Walter said, "We learned through this experience that non-Christian professors were much more curious than we had imagined. They spoke up once they realized they had found a safe place to ask their questions."

Evenings began with fifty-nine-minute open-ended discussions of questions from the participants. All had the chance to express their opinions, but trying to win arguments was not allowed. "The point was not to have winners and losers," Walter explained, "but we did try to provide sound answers," sowing seeds of doubt in the casually held agnosticism of some of the professors. After the time was up, conversation continued in small spontaneously formed groups over dessert. These evenings were fun for both guests and hosts—according to guests themselves, much more interesting than the typical cocktail party. It was a safe environment for curious guests to ask and discuss penetrating questions without fear of rebuke or criticism. Guests were surprisingly open and interested once they sensed they were really in an environment where they were free to ask any questions they wanted, and to enjoy exchanging ideas from people with very different beliefs without the conversation becoming contentious.

During Dr. Bradley's eight years at the Colorado School of Mines, his First Amendment rights to self-identify as a Christian had never been challenged, despite the fact that only he and Dr. Frank Mathews in the physics department were publicly identified as Christians. Ironically, at Texas A&M University—in the Bible Belt—Dr. Bradley had to educate a range of academic bureaucrats on the fine points of religious freedom at an American university. From the first time he and twenty-three faculty friends boldly signed their names to a full-page ad in the *Battalion* identifying themselves as Christian professors, Dr. Bradley dealt kindly but firmly with all who would deny him freedom of religious expression at Texas A&M.

As well as overcoming the presumption that Christianity was anti-intellectual, Walter and other like-minded people on campus had to deal with some unsympathetic and uninformed university administrators. Ever since the groundbreaking Supreme Court decision that prayer in public schools was unconstitutional, public institutions had grown increasingly wary of overt expressions of Christianity in the public square. In the *Engle v. Vitale* ruling of 1962, the Court had ruled that reciting a prayer in class written by state officials for New York public schools was unconstitutional. The next year in *Abington v. Schempp*, the Court struck down a Pennsylvania law requiring public school students to start the day with a Bible reading. As the years went on, some public university administrators, including some at Texas A&M, adopted increasingly restrictive policies regarding the free expression of faith on campus.

In 1980, the Supreme Court ruled unanimously that universities had to treat religious points of view the same as any other. This meant that administrators could not deny Christians or Christian groups rights that were extended to any other students or student groups. Nonetheless, people outside Dr. Bradley's department insisted that separation of church and state required him to keep quiet about Christianity in a university setting. This was not the freedom of expression he and other Christians were guaranteed, nor was it consistent with the notion of a university being an open marketplace of ideas and free inquiry.

In 1987, when Walter and his colleagues first petitioned TAMU administration to become a recognized Christian faculty group on campus, their petition was declined because the university recognized only student groups at that time. As Walter noted, "That was legal since no secular faculty groups had been recognized either. But by 1992, the administration had recognized a women's faculty group, a Hispanic faculty group, an African American faculty group, and there was a petition pending to recognize a lesbian faculty group. If they allow any other faculty affinity group to be recognized, they are legally required to give the same privilege to Christians. The First Amendment requires that the role of the state has to be neutrality, not hostility."

Some TAMU administrators insisted that religious expression was a violation of the constitutional separation of church and state. Walter saw this stance as "a terrible misreading of the Bill of Rights." Patiently but firmly he repeatedly set them straight. "Separation of church and state only means that the state does not give privilege to support and affirmation to churches and religions groups of any kind," he observed. "They simply can't treat them badly either. The people in the legal office at Texas A&M understood that, but the knowledge didn't trickle down."

After Dr. Bradley and the other interested faculty members subsequently appealed to the university president and the university legal office, a Christian faculty group was recognized immediately. Recognition of the Christian Faculty Network in 1993 yielded multiple benefits, including resolving once and for all the legitimacy of their presence on campus.

During his years at Texas A&M, Dr. Bradley had three other of what he called "major head-butting sessions" with deans or other higher-level administrators who challenged the legality of his behavior on campus. "I don't know that they were hostile, though some of them might have been," Walter said. "Part of it was just ignorance. Somebody would complain and say, 'Oh, these Christians can't have a lunchtime Bible study in a conference room. That's using university facilities for a religious meeting. That must violate separation of church and state.'"

Each of the encounters Walter had with administrators was, he explained, "a classic example of policies that violated the neutrality requirement, effectively creating a hostility to Christian professors at TAMU." Christians, Bradley observed, have to be able to hold the line and say, "Nope, we're not going to put up with that."

The first instance occurred when a dean of engineering told Walter he was in trouble for using a sheet of mechanical engineering letterhead to write an invitation to professors to attend a luncheon sponsored by the university-recognized Campus Crusade for Christ student group, for which Bradley was the official faculty advisor. Students then copied the invitation at their own expense and sent them to their professors. One professor apparently complained that this violated separation of church and state. The upper administration contacted the dean of engineering and instructed him to "chastise" Dr. Bradley about this violation. The dean offered to drop the matter if Bradley promised not to do it again.

However, the Supreme Court in 1981 had rendered a 9–0 decision in a similar case at the University of Kansas, Kansas City, indicating that Christian student groups must be subject to the same policies as secular groups. Dr. Bradley asked his dean to get a written legal opinion on the matter. The dean received a stinging response from the TAMU legal department confirming Walter's position on the issue. "People in the legal office didn't want to write some stupid letter that they would have to have to defend in court," Walter said. "They knew what we were requesting to do was perfectly legal and if they refused we could sue their butt off!"

Two years later, a friend of Walter's in another department posted a card on an industrial engineering bulletin board inviting professors to a lunchtime Bible study in the department's conference room. Someone complained to the same dean, who sent a memo to all four hundred professors in the College of Engineering saying it was impermissible to hold religious meetings in any building in the College of Engineering. "I forwarded the memo to the legal office requesting an opinion," Dr. Bradley said. Again the dean was countermanded by the legal department. Unless all groups were prohibited from meeting in the room, the dean could not prohibit Christian groups from meeting there.

Several years later, an associate provost sent a memorandum to all 2,500 professors at TAMU that professors were not to discuss religion or proselytize in class. Bradley immediately visited the associate provost, who was a friend, to thank him for this rule, which would put an end to all the Christian bashing and the promotion of atheism in class. There was a long and pregnant pause, after which the administrator said he did not know there was a problem "both ways," a statement both of them knew was false. Dr. Bradley said he would be glad to collect one thousand or more formal complaints during the semester against Christian-bashers, an offer the administrator realized Dr. Bradley could probably deliver on.

Dr. Bradley asked whether the complaints that led to the administrator's memo came from students or from atheist professors about the Christian faculty group. With some embarrassment, the associate provost admitted that complaints had come from two atheist professors. Two days later he sent out a second memo rescinding the first and reminding professors that they should be sensitive to the beliefs of their students in class. Walter subsequently suggested that the two complaining atheists, along with four other atheists, meet with him and five other Christian professors to discuss the issue. "Sadly but not surprisingly," Dr. Bradley said, "the two atheist professors were not interested in any such meeting." Reflecting on the episode Bradley later added, "Religion comes up in history, psychology, and other academic contexts. It is our first liberty.

To censor Christian history is misleading and promotes an incorrect and hostile view."

In the midst of these battles and his work obligations Walter Bradley reserved time for his family at home. Even during this busy season of his life, he seldom brought work home at night or on weekends. Meanwhile, in the Bradley household Sharon and Steve were growing up. Two of the lessons they remember most vividly from those years are that travel was exciting fun and that money was to be handled carefully.

After the Bradleys moved from Colorado to Texas they went back to Colorado snow skiing every year as Walter had promised. The family spent more time and money on travel than anything else, though the children remember their friends staying at Holiday Inns with swimming pools and putt-putt golf, while they stayed at bare-bones Motel 6's in transit but stayed in nice condos once they got to the ski resorts. The children had taken four trips to Europe by the time they completed college. Sometimes the whole family accompanied Walter overseas for a conference. After the conference was over, they would rent a Volkswagen popup camper and drive from one country to the next for a couple of weeks. As was his habit, Dad never planned ahead or made reservations. Fortunately, they could set up the camper almost anywhere in camping sites.

Walter was as frugal with other people's money as he was with his own. When Steve was in junior high he loved going with his dad to conferences. Steve remembers that they didn't stay in the conference hotel even if the university was paying for it. They would find a cheaper place and walk a mile or two back and forth to the conference every day. Another detail Steve remembers from those days is the difference in asking his dad and his mom for lunch money. "Mom would give me twenty dollars," Steve recalled. "Dad would give me five. He wasn't being mean about it. Five dollars is all you should need for lunch."

Though none of Steve's friends in junior high was a Christian, that didn't stop his dad from rounding up the neighborhood children in his camper van on Sunday mornings and carting them all off to church. He made sure Sharon and Steve had opportunities to minister to their friends. Far from taking offense, the neighbors loved it. "Your parents were golden," one of them later told Steve.

In Colorado, Walter had moved his family from their first house to a second, smaller one that was less expensive and more economical to maintain. In College Station the family lived in a modest house that was one of the smallest of any of their friends'. Dr. Bradley couldn't have cared less. Neither he nor Ann put any stock in appearances or prestige. Steve later commented that because of his parents' spiritual nature they had no interest in impressing their peers. They never worried about having the coolest house or car, or trying to impress people with clothes. "When I was a teenager in high school I didn't like it," Steve admitted. "I wanted us to be cool."

Even if he wasn't cool, Sharon and Steve's dad was thoughtful and kind to them just as he was to his students. A favorite family memory was one time when the children wanted to go to the mall by themselves. Sharon was just old enough to drive, and she and her brother persuaded their dad to let them borrow his car. A few minutes later as they were driving down the road, they passed their father in a suit and tie, carrying his briefcase, pedaling to campus on Sharon's Schwinn bicycle. "He had absolutely no pride," Steve said.

Another car story that became part of Bradley family lore was the tale of Steve's first car. Starting in his early teens, Steve began asking when his dad was going to buy him a car. On Steve's fourteenth birthday, he and his father had a special father/son day. Walter explained to Steve that while he wouldn't buy him a car, he would pay half the cost of any car Steve could afford. After a day spent shopping and test-driving, Steve chose a new red Ford Mustang that cost $8,400. He had two years—104 weeks—until he could get his driver's license, which meant he had to save $40 every week to pay his half of the purchase, $4,200, on his sixteenth birthday.

Highly motivated, Steve set out to get a job, applying at fast-food restaurants and grocery stores. But no one was hiring boys under fifteen years old. Walter, remembering his own job as a paperboy in Corpus Christi, suggested that Steve contact the *Bryan/College Eagle* to see if there were any delivery routes open near their house. Providentially, there was a route available only a block away. Steve started the job, buying his papers from the company, selling to his subscribers, and collecting payments each month. He earned about $50 per week.

While the job didn't interfere with school activities, it required Steve to get up every morning at 5:00 a.m. Even though Walter threw the papers for his son every Saturday to give him a break and the chance to sleep in, Steve still complained about the early hour and sometimes sounded like he was thinking about quitting. When that happened, Walter would take Steve on an errand with him and "accidentally" drive by the Ford dealer to have another look at the Mustang. This would reenergize Steve for several months, until another inspirational visit was required.

Two months before Steve's sixteenth birthday, Walter secretly ordered a new red Mustang with all the features he knew Steve wanted. (While Steve had earned half of the cost as agreed, his dad had to borrow money to pay his half.) On Steve's birthday the family went to celebrate at a restaurant where Walter clandestinely parked the new car outside. Walking back to the family car after dinner, Steve noticed the new car and wanted to take a minute to look at it. Reading the window sticker, he noted that it had all the features he hoped to order in his own car. As Walter recalled, "It was with great joy that we told Steve that this was his Mustang, and he was overjoyed at the surprise. He drove it for three years in high school and four years in college, then sold it for $3,000 to help support a yearlong mission trip to Russia the year after graduating from the University of Texas in chemical engineering.

"Maybe most importantly, the experience planted the seeds of entrepreneurship in Steve's head and heart." He started three successful companies after returning from Russia, and eventually got a PhD in business entrepreneurship to become a professor of entrepreneurship and to have a Christian influence like his father had as a Christian professor.

For his own part, Walter preferred cheap cars even long after he could afford nice ones. (Recently Steve observed, "I buy clothes on eBay and I buy old cars, but I'm not as cheap as he is!") Steve grew to realize his dad saw it as a spiritual issue. Walter would rather contribute to Christian ministries and charities than spend money on himself. According to Steve, his father gives away "well over 10 percent" of his income "and probably always has." Walter was perturbed when cars were no longer available with roll-up windows. It seemed a waste of good money to pay for electric windows when a crank would do the job perfectly well.

The children remember those years growing up in College Station as happy, fulfilling times. The Bradleys practiced "free-range parenting," giving Sharon and Steve a lot of freedom while setting high standards by their own habits and activities. "They were not legalistic," Steve said. "They didn't major in the minors." Like good parents everywhere, they picked their battles carefully. When Steve wanted to drive his new Mustang to Dallas to visit friends when he was only sixteen years old, his parents trusted him enough to let him go. When he adopted "Duran Duran hair and Don Johnson clothes"—referring to the spiky-haired British rockers and T-shirt-wearing TV star of the times—his parents never criticized him. Goofy haircuts were not a moral issue; it wasn't a battle worth fighting.

The children recall many times when their house was full of guests for Bible study, pizza and a movie, discussion and dessert, and other social events, most of them focused on Christian outreach. Their dad liked to invite foreign students over as well, especially at Thanksgiving, a uniquely American holiday. Walter and Ann filled the house with guests on those occasions, sometimes featuring food from India or another country the students were from. Some of the students were surprised to see how small the house was. As Steve observed, the size of their home "sent a spiritual message that there's a different reward in life that's more important than material things. People were impressed by that."

Regardless of the audience or the time of year, Walter and Ann cheerfully spent their time and resources on others. As a young boy among a houseful of strangers on Thanksgiving, Steve remembered, "I just wanted to watch the football game instead of deal with these boring people." But over time the Bradley children learned by example about the value of kindness and hospitality, and learned to see the unending range of opportunities for Christians to share the good news of Jesus Christ.

CHAPTER 8

Success and Surprise

At Texas A&M, Dr. Walter Bradley continued building his record of success in securing research grants in materials science and engineering. Meanwhile, the field of life prediction and failure analysis for metals, plastics, and polymeric composites continued its steady growth.

In 1990, Dr. Bradley accepted an invitation to be director of the polymeric composite materials division of the Offshore Technology Research Center at TAMU, a position he held until 2000. His goal there was to determine the effect of sea water on graphite/epoxy composite materials used in offshore drilling and production. As exploration moved to ever-deeper water, risers that supported offshore platforms became heavier, requiring larger platforms to support them. The idea was to replace steel in risers with composite materials, dramatically reducing the weight of the risers and the size of the platform needed to support them.

At the Offshore Technology Research Center, Bradley could direct research in his field of expertise and also make sure it was beneficial to as many users as possible. This is a role he filled more and more often as time went on: putting scientific discovery to work for the practical benefit of mankind. His research and development work in polymers and polymeric composites was recognized by the Society of Plastics Engineers (SPE) in 2011 with his selection as Professor of the Year (United States, England, and Canada), an award for career contributions to the plastics industry.

Bradley added other academic and professional honors to his list of accolades. In 1991, he was elected a Fellow of the American Society for Materials, a career achievement award given to less than 5 percent of the membership. After twenty years as a member of the American Scientific Affiliation, Bradley was elected an ASA Fellow in 1993. This organization reflected Bradley's interest in the public discussion about science and faith. He explained, "This is a group of Christians who sign a statement of faith that's only five points long and represents basic Christian orthodoxy that most denominations would agree with. Their goal is to help people reconcile what we're learning in modern science and our Christian faith, to see the synergism between faith—God's revelation in His Word, the Bible—and science—God's revelation in His world."

The ASA countered the assumption among some scientists that because we can explain many things in terms of natural laws, this renders belief in God unnecessary or superfluous. "Scientists who believe this are practicing scientism, making scientific-sounding claims without the benefit of empirical evidence, which is the hallmark of scientific work," Bradley said. "Their claims are metaphysical rather than scientific." He added, "I think there's been a big dishonest effort by a lot of atheists who act like with what we know from science today it doesn't make any sense to believe in God," Bradley said. "They think everybody should be an atheist. And it turns out that's just a bold-faced lie. The more we learn, the more difficult it becomes to say, 'Oh, this all happened as a big cosmic accident.'"

In 2005, Bradley was elected to the national board of ASA. He served on the board for five years, the third year as vice president and the fourth year as president. He believed that the impact of his book *The Mystery of Life's Origin* was almost certainly one of the main reasons he was elected to these leadership positions.

In 1995, Dr. Bradley received the Charles Crawford Award from the A&M College of Engineering for outstanding contributions to the college. This award is given annually to one of the four hundred professors in the College of Engineering. Bradley received the honor for being one of the most productive researchers in the College of Engineering and serving in various administrative roles. Though he stepped down at his own request after four years as department head of mechanical engineering,

he served as head of the Mechanics and Materials Division of the department for ten years. He started the Polymer Technology Research Center
and the Blown Film Center while also directing the Composites Division
of the Offshore Technology Center, which was funded by the National
Science Foundation.

During his time at Texas A&M, Dr. Bradley the scientist also found
success as Dr. Bradley the investor and entrepreneur. The year the Bradleys moved from Colorado to Texas, Dr. Bradley bought four duplexes as
rental property not far from the university campus. Over time he gradually added to his holdings. To save money he did all the repairs he could
by himself. When his son, Steve, was old enough, he helped his father
keep the units in good order. In his teens, Steve learned from his dad how
to repair toilets, ceiling fans, garbage disposals, and other items in order
to save on expenses. When the two of them built a fence around one of
the backyards in the hard Texas clay soil, Walter declined to rent a power
post hole digger. Using an auger, they dug every post hole by hand. Walter
would spend money on materials; the high-quality lumber the two used
produced a fence that still stood more than thirty years later.

Overall, Steve later recalled, the partnership with his father "taught
me how to work, how to make money, and how to build residual income."

In 1990, Walter's mother passed away and left Steve a modest legacy.
She had played "a huge role" in Walter's success with her encouragement
and direction, and now had made a thoughtful gift to her grandson. It
was enough to buy a new car, which Steve planned to do until his dad
convinced him to spend it on a four-unit apartment building instead. This
was the beginning of an expanded family real estate business. Dr. Bradley
sold his other properties, bought a tract of land, and built six four-unit
apartments with both Sharon and Steve as partners. As the business grew,
Bradley added more units to their holdings. Steve handled the financial
and business end of the business and took care of managing the rentals,
including the financials and the day-to-day oversight and legwork.

As Dr. Bradley's professional reputation grew, he had far more consulting opportunities than he could accept, so with Steve's help he set
up a consulting business to manage all the inquiries. Steve had returned
to College Station in 1993 to work on his MS degree in mechanics and

materials at Texas A&M and to manage the family rental properties. Steve took on much of the research and engineering for the consulting projects under his father's direction and eventually worked independently. For the next seven years Steve divided his time between graduate school and partnering with his father.

Dr. Bradley arranged his schedule to be available for consulting one day a week, which TAMU permitted. Not only did this allow him to stay on the leading edge of development in plastics and polymers, it gave him a steady stream of industrial examples and innovations to share with his students. When he was asked to appear as an expert witness in a trial, he took a vacation day to fulfill that responsibility.

One interesting case in which he testified involved the Texas Highway Department. As Walter recalled, "The lead lawyer tried to make me look like a cheat being paid by the state to teach at A&M and paid again by the state to testify in court on the same day. I told him to take a break and call my office to confirm that I was taking a day of annual leave to testify, which made the lawyer look really snarky to the jury, like a weasel lawyer." But the same lawyer subsequently hired Dr. Bradley to represent him in another case involving failure analysis, which Walter took as a compliment. "I think subsequently he was elected Speaker of the House in the Texas Legislature."

In another trial, lawyers from the plastics division of a major plastics company tried to browbeat him; they ended up taking a big dose of their own medicine and losing the $4 million case to Bradley's client, primarily as a result of his key testimony.

When Steve Bradley saw his father in action in the courtroom, he saw a side of Dr. Bradley that was seldom on display. "The only time I've ever heard my father be aggressive is as an expert witness against the opposition attorneys," Steve said. "He didn't like the way they tried to twist his words. He's smart enough to beat them, and he does." Steve saw his father questioned on the stand by one of the richest lawyers in America, famous for winning a $10 billion-plus lawsuit in 1987. "Dad had to go against him and pretty much put him in his place."

Walter Bradley vividly remembers the case. "It had to do with a pipeline failure in Pearland, on the outskirts of Houston," he said. A thirty-six-inch-diameter, high-pressure natural gas pipeline that was more than twenty-six years old ruptured and ignited, becoming the world's largest Bunsen burner. The radiant heat from the fire ignited trailers nearby, causing considerable damage to both the trailer park and the residents. Such a spectacular failure and the resulting graphic damage and injury made national news.

"I was contacted by the Texas Railroad Commission, who has oversight authority over pipelines in Texas, to lead the investigation to determine the cause of the pipeline failure, to assign liability in the case, and to give technical guidance to the TRC in order to avoid such failures in the future."

Working with technical experts representing the plaintiffs, the pipeline company, and U.S. Steel, who made the steel for the pipeline more than twenty-five years earlier, Dr. Bradley concluded that the pipeline company and U.S. Steel shared culpability in the failure. The steel had residual hard spots that, when the steel was manufactured around 1953, were probably not understood to facilitate hydrogen embrittlement that could lead to failure. The Cathodic protection system, a technique used to control the corrosion of a metal surface, gave the pipeline company advanced warning that the barrier wrap was beginning to fail. However, had the failure not occurred at a hard spot in the steel, failure by hydrogen embrittlement would not have occurred. Dr. Bradley concluded, "I clearly stated in my report that to me U.S. Steel and the pipeline company shared responsibility for the failure and therefore shared financial and potential legal liability as well."

Dr. Bradley was deposed by about fifteen lawyers in this $50 million lawsuit, including the legendary Joe Jamail, a larger-than-life Texas lawyer who had won some of the biggest court settlements in history against the tobacco industry and against the oil giant he helped force into bankruptcy. He was one of the lawyers representing residents of the trailer park who claimed personal injury or property damage. He wanted to put all of the blame on U.S. Steel, as they had much deeper pockets than the pipeline company. "When he cross-examined me he insinuated that I was lying in my opinion that U.S. Steel and the pipeline company shared culpability.

"He effectively tried to bully me, insisting I answer whether U.S. Steel knew about hard spots causing hydrogen embrittlement in 1953. My reply was that in 1953 I was in the fourth grade and not paying any attention to metallurgical engineering of steel. My knowledge of hydrogen embrittlement came during my PhD studies at the University of Texas in 1968. I said I was not interested in historical metallurgy and didn't know when the issue of hard spots was first understood. Maybe someone else knew, but I did not. My reply abruptly ended my cross-examination."

Steve noted how failure analysis and expert witness testimony gave his dad real-life examples of the fruit of engineering work to share with his students. "He would explain that if we don't design things right, this is what can happen," Steve said. "He would bring examples into class—say a truck axle that had failed allowing a large tire to come off and kill a pedestrian. Normally, engineering classes are all theory, but this was real life. I took his class and he was great. He was really smart but never arrogant."

Another area of expertise for Dr. Bradley was clearly time management, otherwise he never would have been able to master so many varied interests and responsibilities at once. In the 1980s and '90s at Texas A&M, he taught classes in the mechanical engineering department, chaired the department and supervised its faculty, prepared and hosted numerous weekly Bible studies on and off campus, played key leadership roles in Campus Crusade for Christ as a national speaker, launched the crisis pregnancy center in College Station along with Ann and several other couples, spoke nationwide on faith and science topics such as the origins of life and fine-tuning of the universe, built and owned substantial rental property worth about $1.4 million, ran an engineering consulting business, served as president of the American Scientific Affiliation, started and headed the Polymer Technology Center at TAMU, and was awarded millions of dollars in research grants. He also earned his private pilot's license.

"Obviously," Dr. Bradley pointed out, "these things were not all done concurrently or I would have died. I did a bunch of things between 1976 and 2000 but not all at the same time." This incredible list of achievements is due at least in part to Bradley's natural propensity to set goals, prioritize them, and then prioritize his time. Important tasks were at the top of the to-do list, while less important projects were tackled only if there was time after doing the important things well. This process led to him improving his own organizational skills, sharing those techniques with others, and then developing programs of his own to fit the needs he saw in college and high school students.

During the fall semester of his first year as head of the TAMU Department of Mechanical Engineering in 1989, Dr. Bradley read Stephen Covey's *7 Habits of Highly Effective People*. Its training program was eventually adapted by 350 of the Fortune 500 companies to help employees be more productive and also maintain balance in their lives. It was "very helpful in a general way," he thought of the book, "but not transferrable except to a few highly motivated people." Two years later, Bradley learned from members of his industrial advisory board (vice presidents of fifteen major corporations such as Exxon, 3M, and Texas Instruments who hired A&M mechanical engineering graduates) that Covey himself hosted three-day seminars based on his book. There was also a version featuring videos by Covey that could be hosted by local facilitators.

Dr. Bradley immediately went to one of these seminars in Utah, staying an extra two days to take the facilitators' training. Before leaving, he negotiated the first license for a university that FranklinCovey, the company that controlled *7 Habits*, had ever granted. This allowed Walter to present the *7 Habits* seminar at Texas A&M using their videos and workbooks. "They had no idea what price to quote," Bradley said. "No university had ever asked." Seminars cost $1,500 per person for general admission. For corporations Covey charged a large one-time licensing fee plus $150 per person. Bradley negotiated an agreement for a one-time licensing fee of $10,000 plus $70 per participant. "I think because we were the first in an interesting new market opportunity for them, they gave us a 55 percent discount to be the first university to blaze this trail for them."

To adapt the seminar to the university setting, Dr. Bradley reworked it from three full days to fifteen weekly one-and-a-half-hour lunchtime meetings, "exactly the same time as the three-day seminars if you subtract the break times." The new format was a huge success. "Without any encouragement from me," Bradley said, "my faculty and staff spread the word to their friends in other departments, and we would fill the forty seats available each semester with a waiting list."

For the next eight years Bradley held a seminar every fall and spring at Texas A&M with a full class of professors and staff and a waiting list, always with only word-of-mouth publicity. Dr. Bradley achieved his goal "to see the department become more productive, not by working more hours but by becoming much more effective at work and at home. As a result, the department became much more productive in teaching and research while also improving morale and life balance—'a win-win' in Covey language."

Dr. Bradley also looked for ways to help students manage their time more effectively. During his years as a department head, he had a steady stream of students coming by for advice or his approval and signature on some paperwork. He always took the opportunity to ask them what they would change about the mechanical engineering program to make it better. The most common suggestion was, "Give less homework!" But, as Walter explained, "I would always tell them that the problem isn't how much homework we assign—it was required for you to learn enough to pass a professional engineer licensing exam. The problem was how inefficient students are in getting it done." From his research for NASA and the Air Force and from his experience as an expert witness in court, he knew only too well that bad engineers were dangerous and unacceptable.

The freshman year in engineering was especially hard. The tough curriculum weeded out students who couldn't or wouldn't work to grasp the foundational material. Rather than waste more time on a degree program that did not match their skills and interests, it was better to change majors early on.

Still, Dr. Bradley sympathized with students who struggled with their schoolwork. He himself had been relatively lax in his study habits in his first years at college. "I can't give you less to learn," he told his students, "but I'll do anything I can to help you learn it. I'll work you hard, but I'll work harder to help you." Dumbing down the material was never an option. "People learn from failure," Bradley said, "not through phony successes." Dr. Bradley added, "It's good to learn from your mistakes, but it's better to learn from someone else's mistakes." Having discovered how to get through college successfully with a minimum of stress, he wanted to share what he knew with his own students.

Seeing how the information in *7 Habits* helped his faculty and staff, Bradley set out to develop a program for students embodying some of the same principles. He put together a six-hour seminar titled "Time Management and Study Skills for Students." The cost was a nominal ten dollars. "The day after we mailed out fall semester grades to the parents of my mechanical engineering students, we mailed an invitation for students to attend the seminar. I was pleased to have two hundred students sign up for the first one, even though many were there because their parents made them go. But 97 percent indicated on an end-of-semester survey that they were very glad they had come and felt sure that they would do better in the coming semester. And many of them did!" A hundred students were turned away for lack of space. That first year Dr. Bradley reserved a room that could hold six hundred.

Walter repeated his student seminar each year he was department head, then continued the sessions for five more years, opening them up to the entire TAMU student body. Attendance averaged more than six hundred per seminar, with many students reporting remarkable improvement in both their grades and their social lives. Students who took the seminar and applied it raised their grade by an average of one letter grade per class and also had more free time for fun.

The year after Walter completed his term as department head, his children encouraged him to develop an original program to help students manage their time that could be marketed around the country. The result was Success4Students, a daylong seminar focused on the most common problems for college students in using time efficiently and keeping up with classwork. Dr. Bradley's daughter, Sharon Bradley Perry, and her husband, David, organized and executed the first off-campus seminar in College Station, with Dr. Bradley doing the presentations. The Perrys earned enough money to help cover the medical expenses of the birth of their first child, Rachel, one month later.

Based on the continuing success of his presentation at TAMU, Bradley began offering Success4Students at other campuses, including the University of Texas, the University of North Carolina, the University of

Kentucky, and others around the country. Steve handled advertising and the practical arrangements while Dr. Bradley prepared and delivered the sessions. At the first one, between 150 and 200 students registered and paid the participation fee. At the second seminar 400 people enrolled. The enterprise made a tidy profit even though seminars were only offered during the week before fall and spring classes started each year.

"Sometimes family businesses can get ugly," Steve noted in a recent interview. "We never had that. I respected my dad so much, and we were such good friends. I recognized that my opportunities were thanks to his capital and his reputation. We both enjoyed it a lot."

Instead of repeating the seminar year after year, Dr. Bradley decided to create an instructional package for students to use at their convenience and make a video explaining his study techniques. Walter and Steve wrote the script, which had five college students sitting with Dr. Bradley in a coffee shop discussing their concerns. Each student had a particular issue in their learning strategies that they discussed with Bradley and the rest of the group. The comments of the five students illustrated the five main academic mistakes that compromise student learning and academic success. It took forty hours of filming at a movie studio in Dallas to get the two hours of carefully edited program, which was then copied and sold on DVD.

The accompanying workbook helped students follow the lessons and keep track of their success over a twelve-week period of follow-up and self-assessment. It underscored the four goals of the seminar: (1) achieve a 3.5 grade point average, or improve GPA by 1.0; (2) eliminate the need to study at night or on weekends; (3) achieve a balanced, healthy lifestyle; (4) establish habits leading to a cycle of success. Participants also learned better test-taking techniques.

"It takes about thirty days to form a new habit," Dr. Bradley said. "Most students who stuck with the program for a semester were changed for good. The new habits became automatic. On the other hand, freshmen who didn't do the follow-up tended to flunk out or transfer out of engineering."

Walter and Steve soon began to get inquiries from high school teachers who were asked to teach these skills but had no suitable resource materials. In response, a course similar to Success4Students tailored for high school students was developed.

As the turn of the twenty-first century approached, Walter and Ann Bradley took stock of where they were in their lives, what they had achieved, and what they wanted to accomplish going forward. Into this season of reflection came an unexpected opportunity. The national director of the Faculty Ministry, later called Faculty Commons, of Campus Crusade for Christ was moving into another ministry field at CCC. The associate director contacted Dr. Bradley and invited him to become the new national director. Honored by the offer, Dr. Bradley nonetheless declined it, busy as he was with a host of other projects and responsibilities.

Six months or so later, the offer was repeated. Dr. Bradley had had more time to think it over and was willing to reconsider. The objective of Faculty Commons was the same as the objective that led Bradley to an academic career in the first place: namely, to help present a winsome Christian worldview to the secular universities across the United States. Academia was where tomorrow's thought leaders were being trained and also where the Christian faith was most relentlessly under assault. Through Faculty Commons, Christian faculty received the encouragement and training to shine a light into the spiritual darkness of America's college campuses and present the principles of Christ to the next generation of leaders.

Would Dr. Bradley leave his academic post after more than thirty years of teaching and research to go into campus ministry full-time? He was fifty-five years old and at the pinnacle of his profession. What were the consequences of taking early retirement to go in this new direction? With characteristic humility, Bradley recalled mulling over the opportunity.

"I initially said no, I don't think so." But the second time he was asked, after he had a little more time to consider it, Dr. Bradley thought, "Well, it really would be nice not to have to grade papers and write research proposals!" The recollection brought a smile and a laugh. "If I didn't have all that to take my time up I'd have more time for kingdom work."

Bradley continued, "I was at an age and place in my career where I felt like most of the professional things I'd wanted to accomplish I had had the good fortune to do. I was already a full professor; I'd been department head at the largest mechanical engineering department in the country; I was an elected fellow of several national professional societies. I could do more for ten more years, but I decided it seemed like maybe a better use of my time at that point in my life to take the offer."

Walter and Ann discussed it and made the commitment to Faculty Commons. Dr. Bradley took early retirement from Texas A&M and joined Faculty Commons full-time in January 2000. Walter's understanding was that he would serve as assistant director to get up to speed in his new responsibilities. Dr. Bradley would then take over as national director once he had a grasp of the necessary details. After three months on Cru staff in 2000, Dr. Bradley was asked to be the national spokesman for the faculty ministry rather than director.

True to form, Walter Bradley examined his heart to see what God would have him do. "Subsequently," he explained, "I decided that the things God wanted me to do didn't require a title. So I felt like if I had the time to do the things I really wanted to do no matter what my title was, I could do those just as well. Although I was disappointed in one way, I felt like I think this is where God wants me to be and I'm not sure it makes that much difference what title I have."

It wasn't that Bradley meekly submitted to the mistreatment. "It was really not the right thing to do," he said of the director's about-face. Walter was briefly tempted to tell the man to forget it. But he had already resigned his position at A&M and believed in the mission of Faculty Commons. He said, "I felt like God called Ann and me to do everything we could to help advance faculty ministry across the country using what we had done at CSM and A&M as a wonderful prototype of what it could look like."

Considering the new situation in the best possible light, Bradley realized the benefits of having an organization-wide platform for his ideas without the administrative and personnel responsibilities he would shoulder as national director. "I'll be free to travel and speak, and maybe I can accomplish the things I want to just as well," he said. "What was a disappointment at first was indeed a blessing in disguise."

Walter and Ann stayed with Faculty Commons for two and a half years. Though there were frustrations and bumps in the road, these were relatively small impediments compared with the incredible opportunities that developed. "It was amazing how faithful God was," Walter observed.

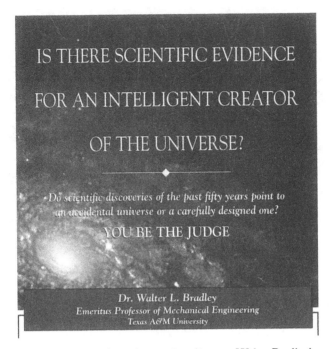

IS THERE SCIENTIFIC EVIDENCE

FOR AN INTELLIGENT CREATOR

OF THE UNIVERSE?

*Do scientific discoveries of the past fifty years point to
an accidental universe or a carefully designed one?*
YOU BE THE JUDGE

Dr. Walter L. Bradley
Emeritus Professor of Mechanical Engineering
Texas A&M University

Ads such as these drew thousands to listen to Walter Bradley's
seminars on science and faith at major universities in the
United States and abroad.

"If we were willing to take little steps of faith, He would do great things." Time and again Walter and Ann hoped God would help with and bless their ministry and, as Walter described it, "God would come through and do something far beyond what we expected. It reminded us to just be faithful, and step back and watch God work."

During those two and a half years as national spokespersons, Walter and Ann Bradley crisscrossed the country working with existing Christian faculty groups and helping start new ones, as well as continuing to develop Faculty Commons and the CCC student ministry at Texas A&M. The couple were eager to share what they'd learned during all the years they worked at Colorado School of Mines and A&M. Walter said, "We felt like what God had done at Texas A&M was so amazing and actually simple at the same time. It wasn't that hard; it wasn't that complicated. It just required some spiritual courage. It was a blessing traveling around

Walter Bradley, far left, presenting his seminar on "Scientific Evidence for the Existence of God" to a packed house at Yale University in 1989.

Pictured is a typical scene after a Bradley lecture on science and faith. After a one-hour presentation and another hour of Q&A at Cornell, curious students and faculty gather and the dialogue continues.

In Saint Petersburg, Russia, Walter Bradley's lecture on the fine-tuning of the universe as evidence for God drew a standing-room-only audience limited to professors and PhD research scientists. (1990)

The Cru team in Russia in 1990. From left, Cru staff member Scott Luley, dancing Walter Bradley, and their Russian host. On the right is Dr. John Walkup, who was the PhD advisor of this book's co-author, Robert J. Marks.

Walter talked at Jinhua University in China on "Thermodynamics and the Origin of Life" in 1988, one year before the Tiananmen Square massacre.

Walter Bradley, on the left on stage next to his translator, speaks to students both sitting on the floor and standing about faith and science in Mexico.

the country and being able to share that with many, many other faculty groups."

Dr. Bradley was invited to campuses across the country to share his own "personal struggle to come out of the closet, so to speak," about being a Christian professor. Dr. Bradley also encouraged his audiences with stories of various "interesting and fun" programs and strategies he and Ann had developed for establishing and extending a Christian presence on campus "in a way that was legal, professionally appropriate, and winsome."

On these visits Dr. Bradley also scheduled talks on faith and science, including one he titled "Fine-Tuning the Universe: Evidence for the Existence of God," as well as revisiting several topics in his book *The Mystery*

Walter on the cover of Korea's *Worldview* magazine celebrating his keynote speaking at the National Korean conference for Christian professors held in Korea in August 2011.

of Life's Origin: Reassessing Current Theories. As many as a thousand people would attend a campus-wide lecture on the topic.

The Bradleys also organized weekend retreats or shorter seminars for faculty during their visits to mobilize them and encourage in-depth discussions, to share ideas, and to support each other. Ann spoke to faculty wives at coffees or luncheons, sharing the strategic role she played in the Bradleys' ministry. Campus Crusade started organizing national Christian faculty conferences that they named A Common Call. Naturally, one of the first plenary speakers was Dr. Walter Bradley. Those gatherings drew five to six hundred professors each. At UC Berkeley, he spoke to an audience of almost two thousand people.

Looking back at his own spiritual journey through the halls of academia, Bradley was amazed at the route his pilgrimage had taken. (A list of universities where Walter Bradley has ministered is in appendix 2.) He said, "It was thrilling to me to see that through the things God was doing—across the country and not just with Ann and me—that I went from not knowing a single Christian faculty member to being able to speak at conferences where we had more than five hundred professors who were there with the goal of trying to take a vision, enthusiasm, and practical ideas back to their campuses to help them impact their campuses."

Bradley added, "It was funny, because the vision I had at the beginning was much smaller than what God had in mind. It was probably good that I only got to see it a piece at a time because it probably would have scared the pants off of me. I'd have never thought I would have such wonderful opportunities."

By 2003, after more than a hundred campus visits across the country and a host of retreats, seminars, speeches, and other presentations, Dr. Bradley began to feel like he had done what he could to help strengthen Faculty Commons and Cru (Campus Crusade for Christ). "We saw a lot of faculty groups improve and do better because they had a bigger vision and more ideas on to how to execute on that vision," he said. And just as he and Ann began to think their work would start winding down, everything changed with a phone call from out of the blue.

PART THREE

A New Season

2003 and Beyond

Following an unexpectedly short detour into full-time campus ministry, Walter Bradley reset his academic and spiritual focus. The offer of a distinguished professorship from Baylor University not only brought Dr. Bradley back to the campus environment, it also provided freedom and a platform to pursue new interests and objectives.

Walter had reached a pinnacle of professional achievement shared by only a handful of distinguished colleagues. By any measure he had earned the right to rest from his labors. But true to his nature, Walter pressed on with a sense of joy and excitement to bring engineering knowledge and Christian outreach to new audiences in new places. Not content merely to reap the harvest of a lifetime dedicated to his career and to his faith, he simultaneously sowed fresh seeds on other ground for seasons yet to come.

As a distinguished professor, Dr. Bradley has helped lead the engineering department at Baylor to develop a thriving graduate program. He turned his skills and attention to engineering solutions that improved the lives of third world communities from Eastern Europe to the South Pacific.

His interests took him around the world. Yet Walter Bradley still encouraged a love of learning at home with his own study skills and time-management seminars. And he stood stronger than ever as a respected and articulate proponent of scientific evidence for the existence of God. His stature was honored through the establishment of the Walter Bradley Center for Natural and Artificial Intelligence at the Discovery Institute in Seattle. Whether there, or building a footbridge in Africa, or defending intelligent design on a national platform, or helping students manage their time more effectively, or hosting Christian study groups in his living room, Walter Bradley continues to write new chapters in the story of his remarkable life and plan a new season of service to his family, his colleagues, and his Creator.

CHAPTER 9

Transition

Walter and Ann made a name for themselves as tireless trouble-shooters and advocates for Campus Crusade for Christ's (CCC's) Faculty Commons at colleges across the country. "We went to a lot of campuses," Walter said. "We got to know a lot of faculty. We saw a lot of faculty groups improve and do better because they had a bigger vision and more ideas about how to execute that vision." The Bradleys shared their own formulas for success based on decades of campus ministry and also cross-pollinated ideas among various campus groups. It was a fulfilling, spiritually rewarding time. However, after more than two years on the job, the couple began to think their mission at CCC was nearing completion. As it turned out, their lives would soon take a completely new direction.

"About the time we felt like we'd done everything we could in that area," Walter said, "Baylor called me out of the blue and asked if I'd be willing to consider coming there." In February 2002, Walter got a call from Professor David Jeffrey, formerly a professor of literature in Canada, explaining he was now the provost at Baylor University. Dr. Jeffrey and Dr. Bradley had become good friends after getting to know each other at summer conferences for Christian professors and other programs. Baylor had hired Dr. Jeffrey, he said, to help with the exciting task of returning Baylor University to its original Christian heritage and raising the standard of academic excellence to a new level. David wanted to know if Walter would consider being a candidate for a new "distinguished professor" appointment in engineering, with the specific goal of starting a graduate program in the School of Engineering, and to lead integration of faith and learning in that department.

Flattered though he was, Walter had never imagined moving away from his family. His and Ann's two children now had six kids of their own, and all lived within a mile and a half of each other in College Station. "I told Dr. Jeffrey I honestly didn't think my wife would be willing to move," Walter said. "It would take a lot to leave where we had lived for twenty-nine years at this stage of life, move to a brand-new place, leave our children and grandchildren, and start over making friends." Though it was only ninety-two miles from College Station to Waco, the move would mean their extended family was no longer just around the corner. Walter and Ann would be uprooted from their many interconnected social and professional friendships formed over the years. "I was thinking this was a dead horse."

Ann particularly loved what she called "cousins camp" every Monday, when all six preschool-age grandchildren spent the day at the Bradley house playing or taking a local field trip in the eight-passenger van Walter had bought especially for their outings together.

But after Walter explained the Baylor offer to Ann, her answer surprised him. "I don't think we should say no without at least going and checking it out," she said. "That might be what God wants us to do." Shocked though he was by her response, Walter agreed.

They went for a visit with open minds. It was their first time ever on the Baylor campus. Walter met with President Robert Sloan, a native Texan and Baylor alumnus with a seminary degree from Princeton who had been president of Baylor since 1995. Sloan had recently introduced a long-range growth plan for the university titled "Baylor 2012." His objective was to transform the school into the Protestant version of Notre Dame, pursuing the highest levels of academic excellence while retaining and encouraging a traditional Christian worldview. Part of his plan was to build a graduate program in engineering, which he hoped Dr. Bradley would be willing to undertake.

The Bradleys' two-and-a-half-day visit ended with a dinner party in their honor. "We were invited to share our personal testimony as the final confirmation for them to make an offer," Walter recalled. "It also underscored for us that our personal testimonies were an important part of the interview process."

While the offer was tempting, Dr. Bradley knew enough about the political intrigue of academia to realize the future success of Baylor 2012 was not guaranteed. During his meeting with Baylor president Sloan, Bradley asked him how old he was. "Fifty-one," Sloan answered. Bradley followed up with, "How's your health?" Sloan replied his health was excellent. Given the political battle going on at Baylor about Sloan's new direction for the university, Walter asked President Sloan how many voters on the board of regents he could count on. Bradley was asking these questions because he didn't want to make the move and then have President Sloan step down in a year or two. Transforming Baylor's culture and direction was going to take longer than that.

Dr. Bradley believed Robert Sloan was a strong and committed Christian who wanted to reverse the trend at Baylor to move further and further from its Christian roots. Bradley saw what had happened over the years at Southern Methodist University in Dallas and Texas Christian University in Fort Worth, where these committed Christian schools had gradually become secular. The offer to teach at Baylor was "a great opportunity to go and start the graduate program, but more importantly to support President Sloan, Provost Jeffrey, and the like-minded Christian professors at Baylor in their goal to return Baylor to its Christian roots."

"I had high regard for President Sloan and Provost Jeffrey and the new direction they were taking Baylor," Walter said. "I was excited to be a foot soldier for them. But I felt that if for any reason President Sloan was not going to be there at least for a sufficient time to get that job well started, then it wasn't worth me going."

The couple discussed their visit during the ninety-minute drive back to College Station. "We agreed that God was surely calling us to Baylor for our last big venture in marketplace ministry," Walter said. "Ann said, 'I think this is where God wants us to be,' and I said, 'I think you're right.'"

Walter accepted their offer and immediately began making plans for the upcoming fall semester four months away.

It turned out that refusing the offer because they wanted to be near the grandchildren would have been a mistake. Within about a year, both of the Bradleys' children and their families moved away from College Station. Sharon and her family went to Austin, and Steve and his family relocated to Indiana. Reflecting on the situation, Walter said, "If we'd stayed there saying, 'You know, God, You're asking too much of us; we can't leave all of our grandchildren,' we'd have passed up this very interesting opportunity only to find that no, that was what God really had in mind. He knew everybody was leaving. It was one of those wonderful examples where God calls us to do things that seem like a sacrifice in the short run when the truth of the matter is that in God's bigger scheme of things it's for our best."

Dr. Bradley quickly formed opinions about Baylor's mission. In his view, the heart of the problem at Baylor was that a professor's commitment to the Christian faith was not a high priority in the hiring process. For a Baylor education to be distinctive from the education a student could receive anywhere else, professors needed to hold a Christian worldview. Some professors argued that if Baylor limited its hires only to committed Christian faculty, they could not attract and hire the best people. But Dr. Bradley thought this claim was ridiculous, and wrote a letter saying so that was published in the *Waco Tribune*.

He argued that the only way Baylor could hire professors from other more academically prestigious universities was by taking Baylor 2012 seriously. Those goals included integrating faith and learning, which only serious Christians could do. In his letter, Dr. Bradley wondered why any professor who wasn't a serious Christian would apply to Baylor in the first place. The answer, he suggested, was because they couldn't get a job in the state at Texas A&M or the University of Texas. He added that such a Christian commitment was the only reason he himself considered coming to Baylor after his distinguished career at A&M. Dr. Bradley noted that seven distinguished professors had been hired recently. Like Bradley, none of them would have had any interest in Baylor without Baylor 2012.

Dr. Bradley helped organize a group of professors at Baylor who then ran ads in the school newspaper, the *Baylor Lariat*, expressing their strong support for Baylor 2012. "Ironically," Dr. Bradley later said, "as a Christian at an aspiring Christian university I developed more enemies in two years than I ever did at secular Texas A&M in twenty-four years."

The Baylor 2012 initiative combined investment in new buildings and facilities with a commitment to active research that informed great teaching. The objective was to increase Baylor's academic excellence in graduate research over several disciplines that would also enhance the quality of undergraduate teaching. The parts of Baylor 2012 most relevant to Dr. Bradley were approval of new master of science degrees in mechanical engineering and electrical engineering, and a master of engineering degree in mechanical and electrical engineering. However, at a meeting of the board of regents where the new degree programs were approved, Robert Sloan had to endure a barrage of withering fire from regents who disapproved of his ambitious new plan.

From Walter's perspective, the regents were supportive of Sloan's plan until they realized there was "more dissention on campus than they had thought. The previous administration at Baylor had not carefully explored the faith commitment of most of the people hired in the preceding fifteen years." A significant subset of professors at Baylor either did not take their faith seriously or wanted that faith to be safe and secure in what Walter described as "the upper story of their intellectual house." But this attitude disqualified their Christian worldview perspective from being included in the vigorous debates about faith and its relevance to modern culture.

Walter noted that this point is powerfully made by Francis Schaeffer in his books *Escape from Reason* and *The God Who Is There*. Religion that remains on that "upper shelf" of intellectual thought and discourse is "safe but irrelevant," Walter said. Both Robert Sloan and David Jeffrey were committed to helping Baylor students—and professors as needed—develop a robust and relevant Christian worldview that could thrive on the "lower shelf," where most intellectual dialogue takes place; a Christianity that can be lived out every day in real-world situations. Unfortunately, resistance to this new focus on faith from some of the faculty and regents was fierce and unyielding.

When he was considering accepting the position at Baylor, Bradley had asked President Sloan what kind of support he specifically had on the board of regents. Sloan believed the board was with him by a count of 28 to 7. That sounded safe to Bradley. But "after about three years of a lot of controversy, publicity in newspapers, even the *New York Times*, some of the board decided they wanted peace at any price and were going to vote to eliminate Sloan."

On May 14, 2004, after rumors circulated that an anti-Sloan group of regents had succeeded in ousting him as president, the board of regents announced that Sloan and Baylor 2012 had won a vote on the issue by the narrowest of margins, 18–17. At a later meeting in July, the same one where the new engineering degrees were approved, Sloan and Baylor 2012 initially received a strong vote of support from the board. Unfortunately, their evident agreement was more wavering than President Sloan realized.

From his position on the inside, Dr. Bradley had a more detailed knowledge of events as they had unfolded. He learned the board was initially split 18–18 about whether to move forward with Baylor 2012. Then, by an 18–17 vote, the board of regents decided to fire President Sloan. By the same 18–17 vote, they selected an interim president who was also anti-Baylor 2012. His first day on the job, the interim president fired Provost David Jeffrey. It appeared that Baylor was going back to its old game plan.

The board suddenly decided to reconsider its number of members. All bets were off. The board scheduled a vote on downsizing from thirty-six regents to twenty. No one would leave immediately; members would rotate off when their terms were up and not be replaced. Downsizing the board was controversial because the first people scheduled to leave were for the most part against Sloan and Baylor 2012. Therefore, board members who wanted to leave Baylor as it was and ditch Baylor 2012 were against downsizing the board; people who supported Sloan and the new initiative were in favor of downsizing.

"There was one regent who was a swing vote," Bradley was told, adding that he heard from a reliable source that this regent received "a very hateful, awful email sent out by people that were supporting getting rid of Sloan." The un-Christian tenor of this email so offended this regent that the regent changed his vote on downsizing the board. As a consequence of this vote change, the regents voted 18–17 to go forward with downsizing. As a result, the board of regents gradually formed a solid majority to move forward with Baylor 2012, even through President Sloan and Provost Jeffrey were victims of the earlier vote.

Over time, as members rotated off the board and the pro-change side increased its majority, three-quarters of the remaining members were very supportive of Baylor being a genuinely Christian university dedicated to the integration of faith and learning. The new board charted a path forward that would, as Walter said, show "how a Christian worldview is significant in many different academic subjects that are taught and researched at Baylor and how such a worldview allows Baylor to become a real Christian think tank and a genuinely Christian place."

To Dr. Bradley, the board action to downsize itself "essentially guaranteed that even though Sloan had already been fired, the board was going to change dramatically in favor of moving forward. It did and it has. Otherwise," he added with a laugh, "I would have been there for a very short time."

The university began recruiting outstanding professors from top universities who never would have made the move without the promise of Baylor 2012. Dr. Bradley noted that it was "an interesting proposition for people like me who had already had a great career at a major university." Baylor's commitment to becoming not only an academically excellent but also a genuinely Christian university made it "a great way to go and invest my last ten years after I had already retired at A&M and had my time with the Faculty Ministry of Campus Crusade for Christ."

Robert Sloan officially resigned as president of Baylor University in 2005. After serving one year there as chancellor, he left to become president of Houston Baptist University. During Dr. Bradley's first exploratory visit to the Baylor campus, he had seen an ambitious and appealing master plan for the future. He also saw that Dr. Sloan was the originator and driving force behind it and was convinced that Dr. Sloan would be at Baylor for the long haul to put his plan into action. Although that turned out not to be the case, Baylor 2012 did move forward under new leadership, and Dr. Bradley was still able to help make improvements to the engineering department and to other aspects of campus life that produced significant long-term benefits.

Over his years in the classroom Walter had seen a deterioration in students' study habits, preparedness for college, and attitude. In some cases it was almost as if students expected good grades without making the required effort. One Baylor freshman came into Dr. Bradley's classroom at the end of the day in tears because of her poor grades. "But I'm an A student!" she declared. She wouldn't be an A student, Dr. Bradley explained patiently, until she was willing to spend two hours studying outside of class for every hour of class time. As Dr. Bradley later recounted, "Two hours outside of class for each hour in class is a forty-five-hour per week load. Surely having evenings and weekends off should provide plenty of time for social life. I told her that she could pull her C- grade in my class up to a B if she would spend the six hours per week outside of class that I recommend for success in my class. She started crying and left my office. Apparently her overly active social life left less than six hours per week for each of her classes."

The idea of investing that amount of time in schoolwork was absolutely unfathomable to her. "Students' general lack of initiative and study time has grown with the spread of cell phones and social media," Dr. Bradley noted. "The internet sweeps up vast amounts of time that could have been spent keeping up in engineering class—time that can never be recovered. Poor time management has become an epidemic as online browsing and communication absorb more and more time." Dr. Bradley could only help students who were willing to help themselves by heeding his advice.

As always, at the same time he was building the new graduate program at Baylor and encouraging a new generation of cell phone–addicted students in their study habits, he was also busy with a variety of other pursuits. Throughout the transition to a distinguished professorship at Baylor, Dr. Bradley continued speaking about the origin of life and fine-tuning of the universe as evidence for an intelligent creator. Around the same time he was settling into his new role as one of two featured speakers (the other was Dr. Michael Behe, one of the driving forces behind the intelligent design movement) at Science Speaks 2003, a symposium on intelligent design in Orlando held in January 2003. It was representative of the presentation Bradley had by this time made more than a hundred times. A video recording of his remarks that day showcases Bradley's skill as a master communicator.

Although by that time Dr. Bradley had been speaking on the mysteries of creation for nearly twenty years, the approach was as fresh and energetic as if he were presenting his thoughts for the first time. He had just turned fifty-nine, but could have passed for a man in his mid-fifties or younger. His round face was clean-shaven, his dark hair short and conservative to match his blazer and button-down shirt. But there was nothing stiff or off-putting at all about his demeanor. He smiled easily and took a conversational tone from the start, thanking his hosts for inviting him so he could follow through on a promise to take his grandchildren to Disney World.

Though he based his talk on the general argument from the book he co-authored in 1984, *The Mystery of Life's Origin: Reassessing Current Theories*, he was quick to update the discussion. He mentioned feature articles in *Time* (1992) and *Newsweek* (1998) about the growing evidence that life in the universe was too complex to have been some sort of random cosmic accident. In years past there was a debate over the importance of designoids, items that appeared manmade but were actually random accidents. Bradley's example was a rock formation in Hawaii that, when the sun was at the right angle, cast a shadow that looked like a profile of President Kennedy. It gave the impression of intelligent design even though it was the result of natural processes. However, Mount Rushmore in South Dakota, with its images of Presidents Washington, Jefferson, Lincoln, and Teddy Roosevelt, is clearly the result of intelligent agency, being carved in minute detail (including Roosevelt's glasses and Lincoln's mole), and is well beyond the creative agency of wind and rain. The chance that some intelligent force carved them is the only reasonable conclusion. As he had said in his book and in the years since, our universe is too perfectly formed and the parameters for success too narrow to accept the notion that it could have happened by chance.

The most important scientific discovery in favor of intelligent design, Bradley explained, was proof of the Big Bang, the idea that the universe began as a massive explosion 4.5 billion years ago. The Big Bang was proven by observations from the Hubble space telescope and information gathered by the Cosmic Background Explorer (COBE), a satellite launched by NASA in 1989 to measure cosmic background radiation. In 1992, scientists announced that without a doubt the universe began with the Big Bang. This was the final nail in the coffin for the steady state theory, which had held that the universe had always existed and had remained constant since the beginning of time. Now, if the universe was created by a massive explosion, something had to have created it. All effects in nature are the consequence of sufficient causes.

Copernicus, Galileo, Kepler, and Newton all believed God created the universe. Finally modern science had to admit that maybe He did.

As Dr. Bradley had done in *The Mystery of Life's Origin*, he detailed the incredible precision required to produce a world that would sustain life in any imaginable form. There had to be a universal element to connect other elements and produce living forms—in our case, carbon. There had to be a universal solvent that was in liquid form—for us, water. There had to be a source of energy and the masses of electrons and protons, but not too much. The speed of light, the force of gravity, and other constants had to be precise to an unimaginable degree. The balance between the forces that bind subatomic particles together, or the electromagnetic force, which holds electrons in their orbit around a nucleus, had to be extremely accurate as well.

As he had in his book, Dr. Bradley used the metaphor of a car engine. The engine doesn't violate any laws of nature, but it cannot be explained by laws of nature alone. Some intelligent force designed and built it. In the same way, life in our universe cannot be explained by nature alone. This does not prove that God exists. Science cannot prove or disprove the existence of God. But it strongly suggests that absent some creative force outside nature, the world we know could not exist.

For Christians the lesson is obvious. With a smile, Dr. Bradley closed his presentation by repeating his belief that in the face of modern science, it takes more faith to be an atheist than to be a Christian. He closed with a quotation from the apostle Paul: "For his [God's] invisible attributes, that is, his eternal power and divine nature, have been clearly seen since the creation of the world, being understood through what he has made. As a result, people are without excuse" (Romans 1:20).

The applause was warm, extended, and heartfelt.

CHAPTER 10

Footbridges and Coconuts

By the time Dr. Bradley joined the Baylor faculty in 2003, he had been a college professor for thirty-two years. He had earned a worldwide reputation as an expert on high-performance graphite epoxy composites, as evidenced by invitations he had received to speak at international conferences in Japan, China, India, Great Britain, and Switzerland. He had published more than 150 papers in peer-reviewed scientific journals and conference proceedings and had been awarded more than $6 million in research funding. Bradley was also a renowned consultant and in high demand as an expert witness in the area of failure analysis and product liability, which was a practical application of his work in materials science and engineering.

Dr. Bradley's reputation, his position as a distinguished professor of engineering, his undiminished enthusiasm for teaching, and his leadership in establishing graduate programs in the school of engineering at Baylor would in time help increase the number of students graduating each year from the engineering department from around 45 in 2003 to around 130 in 2009. Dr. Bradley launched a master of science and masters' degree programs in mechanical engineering that established the foundation for the PhD program in ME at Baylor beginning in 2003–04.

Ann and Walter kept their house in College Station the first three years he was on the Baylor faculty. They wanted to make sure the new opportunity was worth moving for before investing in a new home. The first year Walter arranged his schedule to teach Monday through Thursday, working ten or more hours a day. The Bradleys stayed in a hotel across the street from the Baylor campus Monday through Wednesday nights, then returned to College Station every Thursday evening. The second year the couple rented an apartment in Waco near Baylor where they stayed from Monday morning to Friday evening. The apartment complex was full of Baylor students who, Walter said, "kept their distance, wondering why someone in our age group would choose to live there." The Bradleys still went home to their old house every weekend.

The third year Ann and Walter offered to try something new at Baylor: a professor and spouse living in a dormitory as dorm "grandparents." They proposed to the director of housing, Dr. Frank Suschak, that they move into one of the newest dorms that was laid out as apartments rather than conventional dorm rooms. Walter explained that their idea was "to provide spiritual and intellectual enrichment and also catalyze some wholesome social opportunities." They wanted to be dorm grandparents, not parents. Their role would be enrichment, not enforcement.

Walter and Ann visited the campuses of Rice University and Yale, both of which had had similar dorm parents for years. After meeting with housing directors, dorm parents, and residents, they returned to Baylor encouraged about the possibilities.

Dr. Suschak enthusiastically approved the Bradleys' plan, and Ann and Walter moved into their new quarters in the summer of 2006. It was a women's dorm, which gave Ann many opportunities to teach Bible studies and spend time with young residents who needed mature counseling and advice. Walter tutored residents in physics and other math and science subjects. He also gave seminars in Christian apologetics for the women and any of their male friends who wanted to strengthen their faith or to come to Christianity for the first time.

Repeating their successful movie-and-conversation evenings from the past, the Bradleys hosted showings in their apartment of *Crimes and Misdemeanors* and other films followed by robust discussion around three questions: (1) What question about life did this movie raise? (2) What answer did the movie give? (3) Do you agree or disagree, and why? The evenings encouraged students to think more deeply about the differences between a Christian worldview and the contemporary cultural worldview. "We enjoyed it as much as they did," Walter said.

Skeptical Baylor colleagues kept a close eye on the dorm experiment. "Most professors thought we were nuts to do it," Walter said. "But our year there demonstrated what a wonderful opportunity it was for professors who wanted to have a unique impact on their students."

Today there are six dorms at Baylor with resident faculty couples, and the university has invested significant funds in remodeling each dorm to add meeting space that allows faculty couples (and the students themselves) to have plenty of room for entertaining. All six resident faculty dorms have a long list of volunteer professors and their wives who want to be dorm faculty couples. "The parable of the mustard seed in Matthew 13 comes to mind," Walter said.

A few years later, Dr. Suschak accepted a position as director of student housing at Virginia Tech. There he promoted the idea of residential faculty couples. Today Virginia Tech has three faculty couple dorms with more on the way. In 2008, the Bradleys were honored as the outstanding couple for student affairs at Baylor for their pioneering idea and execution of the dorm faculty couples concept.

Ann and Walter decided that it was time to sell their house in College Station and move permanently to Waco. Steve earned his PhD in business/entrepreneurship at the University of Indiana and later joined the business school faculty at Baylor. Today he is a tenured full professor.

In the meantime, with the goal of integrating faith and learning in mind, Dr. Bradley decided the most effective way to support Baylor 2012 was to combine the two in his mechanical engineering classes. He told his freshman engineering classes that the best reason to study engineering was not that there were a lot of high-paying jobs but that engineers had a unique opportunity to improve the quality of life for others.

Dr. Bradley also brought his Christian worldview to his classes. His last lecture in his Introduction to Engineering class each semester was titled "Fine-Tuning the Universe: Evidence for the Existence of God?" The presentation highlighted the many discoveries over the past fifty years that pointed to a carefully designed universe. To emphasize the point he held up a cover story in *Time* magazine titled "What Does Science Tell Us About God?"

At least twenty books published over the past fifty years explored this question, he continued, beginning with Barrow and Tipler's *The Anthropic Cosmological Principle*, published in 1986, followed by *The Cosmic Jackpot: Why Our Universe Is Just Right for Life* by Paul Davies, *The Constants of Nature* by John Barrow, *Why the Universe Is the Way It Is* by Hugh Ross, *Just Six Numbers* by Martin Rees, *A Fine-Tuned Universe* by Alister McGrath, and *Rare Earth* by Peter Ward and Donald Brownless.

In the summer of 2002, just before Dr. Bradley began his work at Baylor, he had read an interesting paper about engineers who were helping poor people in Africa by developing technologies suitable to their circumstances and financial resources. A complementary article by evangelist Rick Warren's wife that summer also made the case for Christians in the West to be more engaged in improving the lot of poor people in Africa, not with a handout, but with a hand up.

These and other similar articles confirmed for Dr. Bradley his desire to radically redirect his research at Baylor from high-performance graphite/epoxy composites for the Air Force and NASA to technologies that would improve the quality of life of poor people in developing countries. Those in third world countries could never be lifted up economically by selling to other poor people. They needed to capitalize on what they had that could give them a competitive advantage and allow them to engage in the global marketplace. But what could this be?

With Baylor's support (despite the lack of available research funding), Dr. Bradley started to "think more carefully about trying to find things that maybe would actually be helpful to some of the least of God's children." He saw an opportunity "motivated by my Christian faith and an opportunity to use some of the gifts and talents God has given me in a very direct way."

A lot of third world countries don't need leading-edge technology like an Apple watch. They don't need a new supercomputer. They need technology that is appropriate for their country and for where their community is right now. The technology ideally should not only be appropriate but sustainable—for example, a product that gives people living in third world countries the ability to run a company and raise themselves out of poverty. It's the old idea that you don't give people fish; rather, you show them how to fish for themselves.

Dr. Bradley's first foray into engineering for the developing world redirected his attention from graphite composites to the humble coconut. The roots of his interest in coconuts went back ten years to his initial meeting with an ambitious young student from a place where both coconuts and poverty were widespread.

John Pumwa was born in Papua New Guinea, an island nation of 8 million in the Pacific Ocean north of Australia. The country is mountainous and primitive. Many of its citizens are illiterate subsistence farmers. No road connects the two largest cities; air travel or a long walk is the only way to get from one to the other. In 1994, Pumwa, the son of a sawmill worker and his wife, was awarded a scholarship to Cranfield University in Britain to pursue a PhD in mechanical engineering. If successful, he would become the first citizen of Papua New Guinea ever to earn this degree. But before he left for England, he met Dr. Skip Fletcher from Texas A&M, who was visiting the local PNG University of Technology and offered Pumwa a research assistantship. Excited about the prospect of studying in Texas, Pumwa returned the scholarship from Cranfield and moved with his wife, Elizabeth, to College Station.

There Pumwa took several courses from Dr. Bradley, who was also on Pumwa's doctoral advisory committee. Though offered a job in Dallas after earning his doctorate, Pumwa followed through on his plans to return to his home country and use his newfound knowledge there. As he explained, "I wanted to show Papua New Guineans that we can make it with these sorts of qualifications and so I became the first Papua New Guinean to earn a PhD in engineering. I hope that others will come up like me in the future, God willing. I felt strongly that if I did not return to PNG and stayed in the US, then nobody else would ever return in the future. I had to return to my beloved country. I strongly believe that nothing we do in life is by accident, but the Creator of the universe is in total control of our life and we just need to have faith and always know that God is in control." John Pumwa remains today the only native of Papua New Guinea to hold a PhD in mechanical engineering.

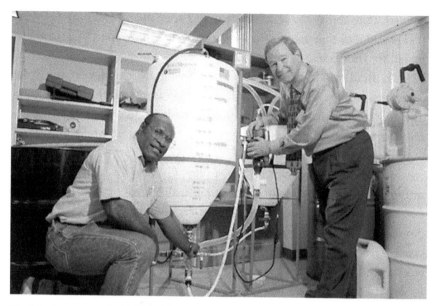

Dr. John Pumwa and Dr. Walter Bradley demonstrating biodiesel fuel made from coconuts (2004).

Six years after he returned to Papua New Guinea, Dr. Pumwa was eligible to take a sabbatical but needed additional financial support. When he contacted Dr. Bradley to see if Baylor might offer a research project for his sabbatical, Dr. Bradley asked him to submit four research topics that "if successful, might help poor people in Papua New Guinea." Of the four, the most interesting to Bradley was a proposal to convert coconut oil to biodiesel. This would provide renewable fuel to generate electricity for isolated natives who lived where coconuts were plentiful but there was no access to electric power.

The project had far-reaching potential. Coconuts were harvested for food and cooking oil, but the husks produced a lot of wasted mass. The broad equatorial belt around the world where coconuts grow is a poor region; except for Singapore, every country has a high poverty rate. Walter observed, "It would seem to be providential that God provided this very abundant but underutilized natural resource in the part of the world where it was needed most." Dr. Pumwa agreed to explore the possibilities of converting coconut oil into biodiesel in tropical rural villages around the world.

With a little trial and error, Dr. Bradley and Dr. Pumwa were able to convert coconut oil into biodiesel using methanol. The fuel they produced worked beautifully in a small diesel engine, its exhaust giving off a pleasant coconut smell. The challenge was that the methanol used to facilitate the chemical conversion process, known as transesterification, was hard to produce in rural areas. However, ethanol was relatively easy to make. The two engineers set out to see if ethanol could be used as a substitute. Laboratory-grade, 100 percent pure ethanol produced excellent biodiesel fuel from coconut oil, but ethanol with as little as 1 percent water "poisoned" the chemical reaction and produced no usable fuel from coconut oil. It was not possible to make ethanol in rural villages with less than 5 percent water content. So unfortunately there was no practical way for local residents to produce their own coconut-based biofuel. Dr. Pumwa returned to Papua New Guinea to work independently on how to turn coconuts into other marketable products.

Meanwhile, Dr. Bradley turned his attention to other possibilities as well. Using his experience in polymer science and engineering, Bradley and his students experimented with using coconut shell powder as a natural functional filler in polypropylene and other engineering plastics. They found that coconut shell powder reduces the cost and improves the stiffness of polypropylene and polyethylene plastics while reducing use of nonrenewable petroleum products.

At the same time, Dr. Bradley supervised a group of five students exploring other possibilities for the 60 million coconut husks that were discarded annually once the coconut oil had been extracted. They found promising applications in non-woven compression-molded fabric for automotive trunk liners and other similar products. The husk fibers could replace petroleum-based fibers. The National Collegiate Inventors and Innovators Alliance (NCIIA) funded their initial research, with subsequent funding from the National Science Foundation through grants to Whole Tree, a company co-founded by Dr. Bradley to develop natural composite products. Whole Tree, later known as Natural Composites, eventually hired several Baylor mechanical engineering graduate students to continue work on these projects.

Over the next two years Dr. Bradley and his Baylor students investigated further uses for coconuts. The shells and husk fibers clearly

Coconut husks, as shown here, produce a lot of wasted biomass in many developing countries.

had potential as components in polymeric composites. Husk fibers, called coir, could replace engineering synthetic fibers like PET in non-woven fabric composites that are also widely used in the automotive industry.

Ford Motor Company saw commercial possibilities in the use of coir to make trunk trim and door panels. The Ford Motors team researching coconut fiber with Dr. Bradley was awarded an Innovation Award from the Society of Plastics Engineers. The compression-molded non-woven fabric composites were initially used in Ford electric cars.

Another major project Dr. Bradley directed was in Kenya, where he led six undergraduate mechanical engineering students in working with the Christian nonprofit Bridging the Gap Africa. Founded by Kentucky native Harmon Parker in 2003, Bridging the Gap Africa builds simple footbridges across dangerous rivers to allow villagers safe, full-time access to markets, health care, and other services. The average footbridge Parker and his team build is 120 feet long. The one Bradley and his team helped build was about 140 feet long.

The bridge in Kenya built by Walter and students from Baylor saved villagers a twelve-mile round trip trek to get from one side of the river to the other.

At Parker's request and with Dr. Bradley's assistance, the Baylor students conducted all the stress analysis to be sure the bridge was safe for up to six people at once. As Dr. Bradley recalled, "We helped him get the right kind of materials, the kind of steel we needed in the cables so they didn't rust and fail in a relatively short time. We specified what kind of wood and what kind of coating was needed. It was a great opportunity to help him—not just to be able to help build that one bridge, but to make sure that this design, which was going to be used to build bridges all over Africa, was safe and properly done."

Speaking of the villagers, Dr. Bradley continued, "People on the far side could not access markets, medical care, or school for their children just across the river without walking six miles down to another bridge, walking across that bridge, and then walking six miles back. Women in the village typically had to go to the market once a week. We calculated after we built the bridge it would save people about 300,000 miles a year in walking. The cost of the bridge its first year in use would be about 0.6 cents per mile."

Parker had been building bridges in Africa since 1997. He partnered with local villagers and enlisted their help with whatever they could do—digging foundations, hauling gravel, and so forth. They also knew about local weather and flood conditions. It was important for them to have a sense of ownership in the finished product. Also, if they helped with construction they would better know how to safely maintain the bridge.

To express their thanks to Dr. Bradley and his team of students, the three hundred villagers on the far side of the river prepared a huge celebration feast. Bradley said, "It was awe-inspiring to know that for $5,000 in building materials we were able to save the women of the village 93,600 miles annually or 1.4 million miles of walking over the next fifteen years."

Dr. Bradley's focus on economic opportunities for the poor created a great deal of interest at Baylor for using technology as part of holistic Christian ministries. Dr. Bradley, Professor Brian Thomas, and several other professors organized a daylong conference at Baylor featuring prominent speakers on appropriate technologies. The conference, held in 2006, was a terrific vision builder for the professors and students alike.

Out of this conference emerged a concept for a national conference on "Bottom Up Approaches to Global Poverty." Dr. Bradley put together a faculty steering committee to develop a proposal for funding the conference through the Center for Faith and Learning at Baylor. The proposal was selected to be the center's primary conference for the fall in October 2008, with a grant of $35,000 plus logistical support. The conference brought together many of the most prominent advocates, authors, and practitioners in the field, drawing more than three hundred off-campus attendees, including some from overseas. Two hundred students and professors from Baylor also attended and were inspired to think outside the box about how to help the poor in developing countries. After the conference, Dr. Bradley received a flood of emails from attendees saying it was the most impactful conference of its kind that they had ever attended, and they encouraged him to host similar conferences regularly in the future. With such encouragement, Dr. Bradley and his steering committee decided to pursue this possibility.

In the spring of 2009, Bradley and his committee put together a detailed proposal for a Global Poverty Center at Baylor. The center's mission would include a biannual conference like the one held in 2008 to provide vision, inspiration, and practical training for people and organizations that wanted to pursue bottom-up approaches to global poverty. The center would also create and maintain websites with appropriate technologies: "best practices" and a website for jobs in these areas. Nonprofit organizations and for-profit companies could post jobs, and people looking for jobs in bottom-up approaches to global poverty could post résumés. This website would then facilitate connecting these people with companies and organizations with the same mission.

This visionary proposal was presented to the Baylor University administration, but they had other priorities at that time.

In 2009, Dr. Bradley and his team of students were recruited by Stan Lazarian, of the Armenia Gospel Association, to build low-cost, well-insulated homes in Armenia. The winters there are bitterly cold, and many poor people live in discarded railroad cars with no insulation. Situated east of Turkey, Armenia is a poor country with daytime winter high temperatures around the freezing mark. Bradley saw that the walls of typical houses of upper-middle class there "are a foot of stone, six inches of concrete, and another foot of stone, and way too expensive for the poor people." The insulating properties of these materials is extremely low. "The thirty-inch-thick walls have an R-value of six, which means they conduct a lot of heat in or out of the place." An R-value of one equals the insulating ability of one inch of solid wood. Depending on construction methods, new American houses today have a recommended R-rating between thirteen and twenty-one for walls.

"We built houses in Armenia using foam blocks we helped design," Dr. Bradley explained. "The blocks are put together like Legos. These foam houses can be built, all the walls inside and out, for about $2,000 in one afternoon. People who cannot afford to buy heating oil in the wintertime need a house that has a very high R-value. These houses have an

R-value of thirty, which says they're extremely well insulated, five times as insulated as stone houses."

Bradley's building blocks, made from Styrofoam, are the best of all worlds: cheap, easy to use, and with a very high R-value—a triumph of innovative engineering for a people who were living in discarded train cars and freezing to death. Bradley said, "When it's cold outside it gets cold inside very quickly. By comparison our houses made out of foam were very, very well insulated. Think of a Styrofoam coffee cup. You can hold hot coffee in your hand protected by only a fraction of an inch of Styrofoam."

Dr. Bradley and his team of students were invited to go to Armenia as part of a larger team to build two model homes in Yerevan, the capital city of Armenia. The two model homes were on national television twice during the week of the build. The idea of a cheap, warm house captured the nation's attention. Within a couple of years, the Armenia government commissioned the construction of 2,500 foam houses in Yerevan. The homes were coated on the outside to make them more durable, and concrete columns in the walls gave them strength. The concept went global.

"It was a fun example, another great adventure I've had the privilege of going on."

The same year, 2009, Dr. Bradley personally helped fund a start-up company named Whole Tree to further develop marketable products from coconuts. One of his partners was Elisa Teipel, who first heard Bradley speak at an America Scientific Affiliation meeting in Colorado. He so inspired her that she attended graduate school at Baylor with him as her master's advisor. "He is beyond brilliant," Elisa said. "His brilliance is more than academics. It's the way he inspires others and cares for others holistically, pointing others to the love of God."

Teipel was one of a host of students who came to share Dr. Bradley's interest in helping poor cultures. There is now a student group at Baylor called Engineers with a Mission, founded by Professor Brian Thomas. Their job is to go to third world countries, identify needs, then develop and deploy appropriate technology. Their first trips were to Africa, accompanied by Professor Thomas with Professor Bill Jordan or Professor Bradley. More recently they have focused on Central America and the Caribbean.

One of the things they figured out how to do was to light houses with battery-powered LEDs. The batteries are charged using solar collectors. The collectors can also charge computers and cell phones, which dramatically improves the quality of life in these areas. They also designed a system with a paddle wheel in the water of a stream that generates electricity to recharge the batteries. LEDs are so efficient that one battery charge can light one of their houses all night or run a computer all day.

Another popular project of Engineers with a Mission is designing and building water purification systems.

They have won the best student organization at Baylor several years in a row. Right now it is the most popular club for engineering students. Every summer they go to a third world country and develop appropriate technology to help the local people. The whole program was motivated by Walter's example. Another former student of Walter's, Dr. Bill Jordan, is doing research into sustainable, appropriate technology using banana fibers. Again, this is a case where Walter's "apostles" are continuing with the work he started.

One of Dr. Bradley's goals in coming to Baylor was to create new, appropriate technologies and to deploy both new and existing technologies in developing countries. Walter commented, "I was blessed to find kindred spirits in Professor Thomas and Professor Jordan who shared this vision and together to create this thriving group of activities that demonstrate how engineers can help change the world. It's worth noting that this has become an excellent recruiting tool for Baylor. This vision of engineers improving the quality of life for poor people in developing countries has attracted a significant number of outstanding students who were introduced to appropriate technology opportunities at Baylor on their visit to campus as seniors in high school."

I (Marks) am at Baylor because Walter called me up and asked me to come. I was thinking of leaving the University of Washington. I had been there for twenty-six years, and it was time to move on. I was hoping to find an endowed chair. These positions are desirable because they offer the recipient more freedom and more funding for research. I was thinking about accepting a nice offer from the Colorado School of Mines.

The contract from Colorado sat on my desk for quite a while. I talked with my good friend Brian Ricci about it. At the time, he was with Campus Crusade for Christ, now Cru. Today Brian is a head of Bridges International, a Cru ministry for foreign national university students in the United States and elsewhere. Brian helped me think through the offer and what I was looking for in the next stage of my life and career and what I could do that would best honor God. I was about to sign the contract from CSM when the phone rang. It was Walter Bradley.

I had met Walter during his visits to the University of Washington, so we knew each other well. I was the faculty advisor for Campus Crusade at the University of Washington for sixteen years and also worked a lot with the faculty to be more overt in sharing their Christian faith. Walter was my mentor in this effort.

Walter graciously said, "I've heard you're thinking of leaving the University of Washington. I'm at Baylor University now. Baylor is aspiring to be a nationally ranked research university that celebrates the lordship of Christ, which would make it the only one in the world that actually did that. We need to get you down here."

He then worked with the provost to get me an interview. I loved Baylor. I was being interviewed as a distinguished professor, and the president meets with all distinguished professor candidates. I met with Robert Sloan, who was president at the time, and the provost, and we talked like Christian brothers and even prayed together. Going to a major university for an interview and praying with the president and the provost was incredible!

I have now been at Baylor since 2003. Coming here was a wonderful experience. I still love it here.

Not long after arriving on campus, I met my co-author, Dr. William Dembski, at an apologetics study that Walter sponsored. Dembski and I, along with Bradley and a number of other professors, were studying a new apologetics book written by Norman Geisler. Geisler had contacted Walter and asked him to go through the book and give him some feedback.

Walter is friends with Geisler, which is no surprise because Walter is friends with everybody. This is when Dembski and I discovered that we were doing research in very similar areas. I was in electrical and computer engineering and was doing work in evolutionary computing: repeating the processes of survival of the fittest, mutation, and repopulation in order to design. Dembski was challenging established assumptions about evolution with seminal works on intelligent design, which made me begin to look at the work I did in a different light.

We started working together and put up a website, EvoInfo.org, on Baylor's server (which I had done many times before), but the dean took the site down. This got the attention of the Christian world, because here was a dean at a so-called Christian school who took down a website of one of their professors. If there was any place in the world where people should be able to freely discuss intelligent design and at least give it airtime, it would be at a Christian university. But that didn't happen. Material on the site included papers subsequently published in prestigious peer-reviewed journals and conferences. Those who censor intelligent design often do not read or understand the material they ban.

I hired a lawyer and went nose to nose with Baylor. We went back and forth. It ended like the Korean War. We didn't sign a peace treaty, but we now have our DMZ and I'm allowed to do all the research I want in terms of intelligent design as long as I mention the work was not reviewed or approved by Baylor. My website was moved off the campus servers and is still going strong today. The president of Baylor at the time, John Lilley, was fired by Baylor's board of regents who felt his leadership was not unifying Baylor after Sloan's departure. The Baylor presidents who followed were open to research in intelligent design, and my work continues without interference to this day.

On a more personal note, my friendship with Walter Bradley was deepened and strengthened by a family crisis that took place about a month after Bill Dembski and I met at Walter's apologetics course. My son, Joshua, broke his neck in a car accident. Fortunately, there was a nurse in the car behind him who rushed to help and kept anyone from moving Joshua until the ambulance arrived.

His injury was the same as the actor Christopher Reeve's. Reeve fell off a horse and broke the same vertebrae Joshua did. Reeve became a quadriplegic. Joshua was more fortunate. He was airlifted to a hospital and fitted with a halo, a metal ring that held his head perfectly still with screws literally screwed into his skull. He moved in with my wife, Monika, and me in Waco to recover. We played endless games of chess, Scrabble, and cribbage to help Joshua pass the time.

When I started attending Walter's apologetics group that was reading Geisler's new book, I came home and eagerly shared the lessons with Josh. After I mentioned my son's interest to Walter, Walter invited Josh to attend. Because of his broken neck and the halo device, however, Joshua was not allowed to ride in a car. There were too many bumps.

"In that case, I'll come to him," Walter volunteered.

Walter made the trip to our house once a week for months to give Joshua a private lesson of the same material he covered in the apologetics class. No one knew except our family. No one can ever say that Walter Bradley does things for the sake of publicity and furthering his fame. This illustrates to me—and I still tear up when I think about it—that he is a devout Christian with a true servant's heart.

Josh eventually recovered and is a high school teacher today.

CHAPTER 11

To Do and to Build

Every Christmas season one of Walter's gifts to Ann was for him to have a physical exam, the gift of maintaining his health in order to be with her and care for her for the rest of her life. His exam the week before Christmas 2006 showed a higher than normal white blood cell count. The doctor ordered further tests. The day before Christmas Walter found out he had leukemia. Still more tests would show what kind of leukemia it was and what the likely outcome was. Two long, anxious weeks passed before Walter and Ann got the results: chronic lymphocytic leukemia (CLL), a form of the disease whose effects vary widely depending on the particular white cell mutation. Lifetime prognosis after diagnosis ranged from two to forty-plus years depending on the form. Additional blood work revealed that Walter had a "17p deletion," the worst mutation possible.

Doctors told him he had three years to live. There were no treatment options.

Up to this point Walter had enjoyed extraordinarily good health, taking only two sick days in twenty-four years of teaching at Texas A&M. The doctor's report was devastating news. The physician, Dr. Christian Cable, suggested they continue to monitor the white cell count and pray diligently that new treatment options would come along in time to treat Walter.

Ann and Walter realized some unexpected benefits as they began to watch and wait. Walter had planned to postpone drawing Social Security until he was seventy in order to receive maximum monthly payments. Now at sixty-seven he applied for Social Security retroactive to his first year of eligibility at sixty-six. The Bradleys used part of this financial windfall to take their daughter, Sharon, her husband, David, and their three children to Israel (their son, Steve, and his wife had children too young to make the trip). "It was truly the trip of a lifetime for us," Walter said. "We sailed on the Sea of Galilee and visited the Dead Sea. I was baptized—again—in the Jordan River. And we spent several days in Jerusalem and Bethlehem."

Walter memorized the Twenty-third Psalm ("for the third time," he points out) and began to meditate on it each morning before getting out of bed and each evening before falling asleep. He said that he and Ann "grew closer to the Lord Jesus in seeking 'peace that passes all understanding' and praying for more than the three years the doctors had predicted." Walter prayed the prayer of Hezekiah, who reminded God "how I have walked before you in faithfulness and with a whole heart, and have done what is good in your sight" (ESV), and God added fifteen years to his life, even though God had said earlier that Hezekiah would die (2 Kings 20:1–6).

Walter came to see each new day as a gift from God; what he did with each day was Walter's gift to God in return. In time he accepted the leukemia itself as a gift in disguise, which, he said, "opened many doors of opportunity to encourage others facing the reality of death and to seek the comfort and peace that only God can give in our darkest days."

Walter, his family, and his many friends prayed for healing. "God answered our prayers in a supernatural way," Walter said. Instead of becoming critical in three years, it took six years for Walter's white cell count to rise to dangerous levels. A count of 10,000 per cc is considered acceptable. By 2012, Walter's level had risen to 180,000/cc. Just in time, a new treatment, Campath, became available. Unfortunately, among its severe side effects was a skin rash bad enough to become life-threatening. Walter's doctor compared it to one of the biblical curses of Job. Treatment was supposed to be three injections a week for eighteen weeks, but Walter's reaction was so strong that after one week he developed skin rashes that would take two months to heal. The good news—miraculous news—was that Walter's white cell count plunged from 180,000/cc to 2,000/cc in a single week.

"Dr. Cable noted two miracles," Walter recalled. "The Campath worked eighteen times faster than expected, and I didn't die from kidney failure due to 178,000/cc of dead white cells dumping into my bloodstream all at once." Dr. Cable asked Walter if his urine had been dark the week his white cell count plunged. Remarkably, Water had seen no change in his urine at all. How all those dead white cells disappeared appeared to be another miracle. "The result was inexplicable according to medical science."

The watching and waiting resumed. Over the next four years Walter's white cell count gradually rose again to dangerous levels, this time 200,000/cc, depressing his red cell count and adding anemia to his health challenges. Then on top of everything else, in 2016 Walter was diagnosed with bladder cancer. Leukemia treatment was temporarily suspended in order to schedule bladder surgery. The first surgery not only failed to remove all of the tumor but resulted in a perforated bladder. Leukemia treatment had to be further postponed until after the second bladder surgery, which couldn't occur for another two months until the bladder perforation healed. Had his white cell count continued to rise in the way it had been increasing for ten years while waiting for treatment to resume, the result would have been deadly.

Remarkably—miraculously—his white cell count dropped 30 percent on its own and stayed at that level until Walter recovered from the second surgery and could resume leukemia treatment. In his ten years battling leukemia, his monthly blood tests *always* showed an increase in the white cell count as they continued to multiply. "That my counts not only did not increase *for the first time* in 120 monthly blood tests, but dropped 30 percent was a gift from God, providing the time needed for my bladder cancer treatment to be completed without me dying from leukemia."

Walter believes God has providentially cared for his health in response to prayers of many faithful family and friends. He said, "I have an account at CaringBridge that has allowed me to communicate to my prayer supporters. The 264 people registered on my prayer support team have sent almost six thousand messages of encouragement. Not only have they moved the hand of God on my behalf with their prayers, they have blessed and encouraged me with their messages. It's another example of how life challenges are often God's blessings in disguise—sometimes very well disguised.

"We are told 'to give thanks in all circumstances; for this is the will of God in Christ Jesus' [1 Thessalonians 5:18 ESV]. I can truthfully say that God has blessed me in many unexpected ways through my thirteen years of battle with cancer. Jesus can really cause 'all things to work together for good, to those who are called according to his purpose' [Romans 8:28 ESV]."

Whatever foothold the disease might have gained did nothing to keep him from taking advantage of new opportunities to speak out in favor of Christianity. True to form, Walter didn't wait for challenges to come to him but went out gunning for them, always unfailingly polite yet unfailingly effective in advancing his position.

Walter has more guts than almost anybody we have ever known. One example of his attitude was his response when he found out there was an atheist group meeting on the Baylor campus. Though faculty members are required to be Christian, students are not. So atheists get in, and they congregate. Walter decided he should go and talk to them.

One of his former students invited him to give his presentation to the atheists on "Fine-Tuning of the Universe as Evidence for the Existence of God," the talk he gave in class at the end of each semester and to many universities across the United States. Bradley spoke to the atheist and agnostic group (not officially recognized on campus) for an hour one Sunday night. About fifty Baylor students attended, most of them members of the Atheist Student Network. Obviously hungry for information and answers, they asked questions for three hours after the presentation. Then they invited him to their next group meeting, grateful for his respectful approach and obvious interest in their views. Bradley accepted enthusiastically.

At that meeting Dr. Bradley invited the atheist and agnostic group to his house for hamburgers and to watch a PBS video called "The Question of God," comparing the beliefs of Sigmund Freud and C. S. Lewis.

To his amazement, twenty students came. The lively discussion that followed went until midnight. Walter observed, "Everyone thought it was remarkable to have cordial conversation on such a divisive topic where every person had the opportunity to share their responses." Before they left, the students asked for a follow-up session. Reminded that final exams were coming up, they wanted to meet anyway. The Bradleys agreed to host and were amazed to have fifteen students come during "dead days."

This outreach set the stage for two years of regular meetings to have cordial and open-ended discussions about, "The Question of God." Ann and Walter learned that many of the students were from very legalistic Christian homes and churches where asking hard questions about faith was not allowed. Some came from atheistic homes and had a second-hand acceptance of atheism from their parents. All of them looked at their positions with new eyes, and many returned to Christianity or seriously considered it for the first time. "Our periodic dinners with these students were one of the highlights of our time at Baylor," Walter said.

Along with outstanding Baylor students, Dr. Bradley and I (Marks) worked to start an apologetics group at Baylor. It was not an easy task, even though Baylor is a Christian university. Formerly churchgoing students often stop going to church after they get to college. Some studies say up to 70 to 80 percent quit going to church. The reason is because the church has failed to educate these kids in apologetics. They don't know how to respond when their snarky professors begin saying this and that about Christianity. Dr. Bradley and I determined that one of the solutions to this problem was to form a group to discuss apologetics.

We had a difficult time getting it approved as a recognized student group at Baylor, but finally we succeeded, and Walter was the genesis of that. He was always there with advice and pointers. It turned out the person we needed to talk to, the vice president for Student Affairs, Dr. Kevin Jackson, was at Baylor because of Walter. Because Walter knew Kevin—remember that everybody knows Walter—we had a meeting with him and explained our idea. Kevin said, "Well, of course we need an apologetics group. Any opposition to that is kind of silly."

The group met weekly and also set up presentations and panel discussions. One fall as students arrived on campus at the beginning of the term, the group held a panel session called "Does God Matter?" with Bradley as one of three panelists. Publicity for the event invited students to come and ask their most difficult questions about God and the existence of God, Christianity, and why Christianity is true. We knew we had to get them in a comfortable situation before we could expect them to ask these kinds of questions. They are almost ashamed to ask them because we're in the Bible Belt, and in the Bible Belt you don't question God and Christ. But you need to. That's the purpose of apologetics.

Of course Walter has never limited his defense of Christianity to the campus. He was known across the country—and to some degree around the world—for his research on questions of faith and science skillfully presented in lectures, book chapters, and the book he co-authored on the origins of life. In Waco, Texas, outside the Baylor campus, he soon added a new mainstream venue to his list: the parking lot of a fast-food restaurant.

It began with an interview given by Truett Cathy in 2012, the chairman of Chick-fil-A, an evangelical Christian who had been unashamedly public about his faith. As Walter recalled, Cathy "said that even though he believes same-sex marriage is wrong, he still hires homosexuals and serves them in his stores." In today's hair-trigger politically correct environment, Walter continued, "this perceived slight of homosexuals resulted in calls for a national boycott of Chick-fil-A. This demonstrates what Christianity is like in the business world." Walter noted that Christians have to be prepared to accept the consequences of standing strong for their faith in contemporary culture.

To counter the boycott, political commentator and former Arkansas governor Mike Huckabee organized Chick-fil-A Appreciation Day on August 1, 2012. In Waco, crowds swarmed the local Chick-fil-A outlets in support of Cathy and his right to free speech. The stores sold three times more food that day than they had previously ever sold in a day. Walter joined the huge crowd of Waco residents that rallied to support their local restaurants. At 6:30 p.m. a line of cars two miles long waited for service. True to form, Bradley couldn't watch passively as a small cluster of ten or twelve protesters marched in front of the location he visited. They carried signs accusing Cathy and his customers of being bigots. Though the crowd of customers ignored them, Walter gave Ann the wheel, got out of the car, and walked over to talk to them.

"I'm curious to hear more about your signs," Walter said in his disarmingly friendly manner. "What makes you think I'm a bigot?" The protestors couldn't answer the question. He began to engage the protesters about what it meant to have an abortion and what it was like to support the pro-life position.

This was a gutsy act. The same sort of gutsy act that Walter did with the atheist group at Baylor. We suspect Bradley's thinking was, "If you see people who are ideologically opposed to you, it doesn't mean they are bad people. They're sons and daughters of God. They just don't know Christ yet. Go talk to them, go minister to them." As department chair at Texas A&M, Walter had 110 employees under him. He thought, "I had differences of opinion with people in the department at A&M. But as a Christian I need to be charitable to people I disagree with. In this case, the people carrying signs were the bigots."

One of the Chick-fil-A protesters claimed there was nothing in the Bible condemning homosexuality. Walter responded with Romans 1:24–27, which tells of men who "gave up natural relations with women and were consumed with passion for one another, men committing shameless acts with men" (ESV).

Dr. Bradley knew that the difference between the protesters and himself was that he believed the Bible was the Word of God and they didn't. "That doesn't make me a bigot," he told them. "Either the Bible is true or the Bible is false. Unless you can prove it's false, you cannot rationally claim I'm a bigot for believing it. I don't discriminate against gays in hiring, socializing, or letting them live in my rental property. Does that make me a bigot? Could it be you're the one who's a bigot? Maybe you should be more tolerant of people you disagree with when there's no proof of who is right. If you want to help your cause, don't do this." They subsequently had a pleasant get-acquainted chat with Dr. Bradley for a few minutes, allowing the conversation to conclude on a cordial note. The protesters left shortly thereafter.

Later Walter added, "The protesters were surprised to be engaged in cordial, rational conversation. They didn't try to argue, as my comments left little to add to the conversation unless they were prepared to argue persuasively that the Bible was not true."

In subsequent discussion with friends Bradley said, "The media today invite extremes. They demonize. We can't sit down and have reasonable discussions about important things. We're going in a direction that's dangerous to our democracy. I look for radicals and ask them questions. It forces them to explain why they take the positions they do. The fact is, they don't know. Their position and behavior are purely the result of groupthink. They don't analyze the issue for themselves, which means they're not good at defending their position on their own.

"We have a tweet level of communication in our culture today even when we're not tweeting."

In all the Chick-fil-A locations in the world that day, there probably wasn't another person who did what Walter did. What a heart for God, recognizing that a true Christian goes to people who need God in Christ!

Dr. Bradley's boldness and effectiveness in Christian ministry has been rewarded. In 2018, as a colleague, friend, and admirer of Walter Bradley, I (Marks) was chosen to break the news to Dr. Bradley that a new arm of the Discovery Institute in Seattle was being built and would be named the Walter Bradley Center for Natural & Artificial Intelligence. My wife and I took Walter and Ann to dinner at the Baylor Club and told them about the Walter Bradley Center for the first time. The response was typical Walter. First he said, "No, no, you can't do this." He knew about my work in intelligent design and said it should be named after me. I responded, "No, I'm not old enough!" and we both laughed. Walter is not a man who seeks recognition, and when it's given to him, he is very humble.

Since its founding in 2018, the Walter Bradley Center has had many diverse activities. The website MindMatters.ai posts articles from Bradley Center Fellows like neurosurgeon Michael Egnor, economist Gary Smith, philosopher Jay Richards, information theory experts like Eric Holloway and Jonathan Bartlett, and software experts like Winston Ewert and Brendan Dixon. Grants from the Bradley Center support cutting-edge research in the origin of life, algorithmic information theory, and appropriate technology focused on entrepreneurship in developing countries.

During dinner on January 25, 2018, Ann and Walter Bradley (left) were first told by Robert and Monika Marks that Discovery Institute's new center on artificial intelligence would be named the Walter Bradley Center for Natural & Artificial Intelligence.

I host a weekly podcast "where natural and artificial intelligence meet head-on." The Bradley Center also supports new books and other writing on natural and artificial intelligence, including an updated version of *The Mystery of Life's Origin* and an edited volume dedicated to the mind-body problem. The year 2019 saw the launch of COSM, an event featuring talks from luminaries like George Gilder, Peter Thiel, Steve Forbes, and Ray Kurzweil, as well as your humble authors. We are working hard to live up to Walter Bradley's legacy.

I (Dembski) have admired Dr. Bradley for decades and was instrumental in inviting him to come to Baylor. I first heard of Walter Bradley as co-author of *The Mystery of Life's Origin*. As a young scholar I checked the book out of a library in 1989. Inspired by what I read, along with other seminal works in the intelligent design movement, including Michael Denton's *Evolution: A Theory in Crisis*, I published an article in the philosophy journal *Nous* titled "Randomness by Design," which took the view that randomness is a parasitic notion that depends on underlying patterns that it violates. This article, perhaps more than any other, put me on the radar of the at-the-time burgeoning intelligent design community.

I found *The Mystery of Life's Origin* to be significant on a number of fronts. First, it took on the weakest link in any naturalistic attempt to make scientific sense of the world, namely, the origin of life. It showed that life's origin is completely unexplained in terms of known or imagined material mechanisms. Moreover, it compellingly raised the possibility of life's origin being the result of a designing intelligence, though without trying to inject religion into the discussion. Rather than argue in favor of religion-based explanations, the book presented arguments for why naturalistic mechanisms could not reasonably be thought to explain life's origin. Bradley focused on design at the origin of life and in cosmology (the origin of the universe), leaving Darwinian evolution to the biologists in the intelligent design community.

A second major feature about the book was that since it had no religious philosophy to promote or defend, it was released in the mainstream secular press instead of a religious publisher. *The Mystery of Life's Origin* was published by Philosophical Library, which had published the work of numerous Nobel laureates as well as notable philosophers such as Martin Heidegger. Walter thus set the stage for the mainstreaming of intelligent design.

A few years after encountering Dr. Bradley's writing, I was invited to participate in a symposium on the origins of life sponsored by the Foundation for Thought and Ethics. Four other supporters of intelligent design and I debated five Darwinists. Walter Bradley was a guest speaker at the event. When he took the podium, I found him impressive: a high-powered, no-nonsense engineer of the highest intellectual caliber. He and I crossed paths occasionally in the years that followed. We both attended a meeting in Pajaro Dunes, California, in 1993 organized by Dr. Phillip Johnson, considered by many to be the father of the intelligent design movement. It was a strategy session that helped define the path for the future of intelligent design.

Walter Bradley in 2001.

In November 1996, Dr. Bradley was a keynote speaker at the Mere Creation conference hosted by Biola University in Los Angeles, which I helped organize and whose proceedings I edited into a book released two years later. Walter's presentation there was a standout example of his public presentations on behalf of intelligent design.

Dr. Bradley contributed to an anthology I edited titled *Signs of Intelligence*, published in 2001. His contribution was a version of the explanation of intelligent design he had been writing and speaking about for decades. It was what, even today, I would regard as the most succinct and persuasive case for the physics of the universe being a consequence of a designing intelligence.

I was a professor at Baylor when the provost there, David Jeffrey, decided to offer Bradley a distinguished professorship at the engineering school. I had the pleasure of making the first overtures to Bradley that resulted eventually in his move to Baylor. In 2005, Dr. Bradley was instrumental in my being a co-recipient of the Trotter Prize for Information, Complexity, and Inference, awarded annually by Texas A&M.

Other recipients have included Nobel laureates Francis Crick (Medicine) and Steven Weinberg (Physics). This prize was a big deal. Walter's good word for me to the Trotter Prize committee no doubt helped me onto this august platform.

In 2010 I first learned of Walter Bradley's interest in helping people in the developing world not only by devising appropriate technologies to help them but also by marshalling the entrepreneurial abilities, funding, and practical skills to put those technologies to work. Although I always found Walter's work on intelligent design insightful and stimulating, I found his work on appropriate technologies inspiring. His work helping coconut farmers turn coconut husks into filler material for floor mats is brilliant in its discovery of hidden value in everyday items that we might otherwise ignore or throw away. I like this about Walter more than anything else: his ability to find value where others are missing it, and using that value to help others. A fruit of his efforts was the formation of Dignity Coconut Oil. The company is run and operated by Philippine nationals in a poorer section of the islands. Dignity Coconut Oil can be purchased on Amazon.com.

With our complementary public profiles in both academia and the intelligent design debate, it was only natural that Dr. Bradley and I would find ourselves together at the Discovery Institute. This Seattle-based non-profit was founded in 1990 to promote discussion of the intelligent design theory of the universe and to encourage scientists and educators to consider and teach it along with evolution and other origin-of-life concepts.

Walter and I were on Discovery Institute's radar separately for our work on intelligent design. As the clearinghouse for the intelligent design community, it was a good place for both of us to advance our work in this area, so it was natural for them to invite us on board. Both of us became fellows of the institute in the 1990s. Resistance to intelligent design in the academy has been strong for the last thirty years, even though isolated supporters exist on the faculties of many universities. Discovery has thus been a mutual support society for ID proponents who might otherwise have easily ended up as—to use the scientific term—roadkill. Walter, as a tenured professor, was obviously in a more secure position than many of us more junior scholars, and it has helped to have his support from that position of strength.

Concurrent with our defense of intelligent design, Walter and I have encouraged discussion about human intelligence in the context of the rise in computer technology and artificial intelligence (AI). We believe strongly that AI has not approached and will never approach the level of human intelligence, and therefore we have no reason to fear it. What we do need to concern ourselves with is making sure we can live comfortably with machines as their master, never allowing them to master us. To that end, in 2018 I was honored to help endow the Discovery Institute's new center for research into natural and artificial intelligence in honor of Walter Bradley.

In remarks prepared for the opening of the Walter Bradley Center for Natural & Artificial Intelligence in Seattle on July 11, 2018, I noted that its purpose would be "to clarify the limits of machine intelligence, to understand intelligence as it exists in nature (preeminently among humans), and above all to chart fruitful paths for humans to thrive in a world of automation brought on by AI."

I continued, "It's really this latter aspect of the center that will define its success and impact. It's one thing to exchange arguments and critiques with the defenders of strong AI. But the real challenge for this center is to help build an educational and social infrastructure conducive to productive human-machine interaction. The point is not simply to talk and critique; it is to do and to build."

The rise of machine intelligence and its entry into every part of life has established a need to demonstrate the difference between human and machine intelligence and how humans will always remain superior. Humanity, I pointed out, is not "unexceptional and even obsolete as some proponents of AI claim. . . . Predictions of human obsolescence are sheer hype. Machines have come nowhere near attaining human intelligence. . . . *[Z]ero evidence* supports the view that machines will attain and ultimately exceed human intelligence. And absent such evidence, there is *zero reason* to worry or fear that they will."

The artificial intelligence community has developed sophisticated algorithms for everything from playing board games to self-driving cars to curating the ads a particular viewer sees on Facebook. But someone has to put that algorithm to work on that problem. What AI has never done is self-select from all available algorithms the best one to handle a particular task. There is no algorithm of algorithms.

As I explained in my remarks, for full-fledged AI to become a reality, "AI needs more than a library of algorithms that solve specific problems. To date, AI has done nothing more than build such a library. But that's hardly sufficient. Instead, an AI takeover needs a higher-order master algorithm with a general-purpose problem-solving capability, able to harness the first-order problem-solving capabilities of the specific algorithms in this library and adapt them to the widely varying contingent circumstances of life. Building such a master algorithm is a task on which AI's practitioners have made zero headway."

What is needed is "a coordination of all these algorithms, appropriately matching algorithm to problem across a vast array of problem situations. A master algorithm that achieves such coordination is the holy grail of AI. But there's no reason to think it exists. Certainly, work on AI to date proves no evidence for it." Therefore, "there's no reason to hold our breath or feel threatened by AI. The only worry really should be that we embrace the illusion that we are machines and thereby denigrate our humanity. In other words, the worry is not that we'll raise machines to our level, but rather that we'll lower our humanity to the level of machines. . . .

"In Walter Bradley, we find someone who has reflected deeply on the intersection of natural and artificial intelligence, who has done seminal research in this area, who has been an educator, who has ever been concerned about the well-being of fellow students and faculty (digital wellness now being part of that), who has advanced appropriate technologies, and who has harnessed these technologies to help people in the developing world make a living. Add to that Walter has been fearless and uncompromising in standing against the materialist currents of our age, and you have a worthy namesake for this center.

"I couldn't be happier for this fitting legacy in his honor. With its skepticism of strong AI (the view that any day now computers will match and then exceed human intelligence), with its emphasis on human flourishing in the wise use of technology, and with its eye on using technology to empower the dispossessed through appropriate technologies and entrepreneurship, this center promises to do the world a lot of good."

CHAPTER 12

Don't Worry About the Water

Everyone concerned about the rise of artificial intelligence can rest easy: no machine will ever replace Walter Bradley. No box full of electronics will ever deliver the smallest fraction of Walter's judgment, kindness, wisdom, resolve, common sense, humility, and Christian truth. None will ever approach his record of success. He has now taken his seventy-fifth birthday in stride, continuing to pursue projects on familiar topics as well as exploring new fields of interest. With his cancer diagnosis more than a dozen years in the past, he focuses with undiminished interest and anticipation on the future.

In recent years Dr. Bradley has put his engineering skills to use on an all-new application. From metallurgy to polymers, from jet fighters and water pipes to footbridges in Kenya and coconuts in Papua New Guinea, Walter had already immersed himself in a vast range of projects. In 2003, the Curves International women's fitness franchise offered him a research grant to use at Baylor for developing their next generation of exercise equipment. In its advertising the company emphasizes its thirty-minute exercise regimen and promotes "safe and effective machines designed especially for women." The equipment is a major draw; Walter came up with new ways to make it better.

"The key to stepper machines is the hydraulic cylinders that provide the resistance," Walter said. "One of the challenges is to design a cylinder that will work as well for women who weigh one hundred pounds as for women who weigh two hundred pounds." The hydraulic tubes in Curves machines provided a linear increase in resistance as the velocity increased. Dr. Bradley intuitively sensed this was backward. "What they needed was a nonlinear relationship between piston velocity and resistance," he said. "When the speed was doubled, the resistance should increase by a factor of four."

Not only did the new cylinders produce a better workout experience, they were less expensive to manufacture. This combination of performance and cost savings gave Curves significant competitive advantages. Dr. Bradley invited several new assistant professors to work on other aspects of the equipment, producing other significant improvements. Walter recalled, "One of the highlights of the projects was getting to fly with Gary Heavin, the founder and then chairman of Curves, on his corporate jet to the South Texas Valley where most of the manufacturing was done."

The Curves project at Baylor is one of many examples of Dr. Bradley's long-term success in securing research funding. During his career Walter attracted more than $6 million in funding to sponsor the research of his graduate students and himself at Texas A&M and Baylor. Funding sponsors included government agencies such as the National Science Foundation, the Department of Defense, the Air Force Research Laboratory, and NASA, as well as Fortune 500 companies including 3M, Dow Chemical, DuPont, Phillips, Exxon, Ford Motor Company, and other major producers of engineering plastics.

Walter was happy he could use research funding to provide cutting-edge research projects for his graduate students along with research assistantships to pay for their living expenses and research equipment. He typically supported eight graduate students at Texas A&M and six undergraduates at Baylor.

Along with publishing in respected academic journals, research funding is a chief measure of professional success. Authors are warned their overt Christianity could hamper their prospects for getting research dollars. However, their faith wasn't a liability after all.

Both Walter and I (Marks) had pushback at Baylor by professors who feared if the university and its professors became too overtly identified as

Christians, they wouldn't get government funding. That might be true in some fields, but it certainly isn't in engineering, because we're concerned with the final output, with what works. If you can show that you can do the work and that the work is worth doing, then people are going to respond.

Walter and I have been very successful attracting external money, despite the fact that we're both openly Christian, and we've been very well supported over the years.

During his first year at Baylor, Walter was invited to lunch by the chairman of the faculty senate to discuss the potential negative impact his identity as a Christian could have on external research funding. Walter replied that before his co-authored book *The Mystery of Life's Origin* was published in 1984, he had been receiving about $160,000 per year in research funding. After the book came out, for most of the 1990s his funding averaged around $300,000 annually. Walter remembered, "I gently tried to point out that for Baylor professors, including the chairman of the faculty senate, the problem was not Baylor's Christian identity but rather the poor quality of their proposals and a lackluster track record of peer-reviewed published research." Those performing poorly rarely examine themselves as the source of failure.

Clearly Dr. Bradley has not only succeeded but flourished as a professor whose professional reputation is closely associated with his Christian worldview. After a long and distinguished career in his field, he shows no signs of slowing down. In September 2018, he accepted an invitation to be one of three plenary speakers at an international conference on materials and manufacturing in Bali, Indonesia, where he shared his research on using coconut shells and husks to make environmentally friendly car parts.

Dr. Bradley was also invited to speak at the Society of Plastics Engineers international conference on polyolefins in Houston, Texas, in February 2019 to present his work on using coconut shell powder and husk fibers to make environmentally friendly automotive components and home siding.

In April 2019, Dr. Bradley was honored to receive the Trotter Prize for research at the interface of faith and science, a $5,000 award given annually to two recipients by the College of Science and the College of

Engineering at Texas A&M. Bradley's award cited *The Mystery of Life's Origin*, which was the first book from a secular publisher (Philosophy Library) to argue for the inadequacy of natural laws alone to explain the origin of life. The book received favorable reviews in various technical journals and garnered winning jacket endorsements from three prominent scientists who were not theists.

In recent years Dr. Bradley has been a plenary speaker at fourteen different conferences across the country sponsored by Faculty Commons, the division of Cru that ministers to university professors, sharing ideas that he and Ann have developed in their forty-four years on college campuses. His first talk at those events takes its title from the book by John Ortberg, *If You Want to Walk on Water, You've Got to Get Out of the Boat*, addressing the most common reason why Christian professors stay in the closet. His second presentation is "On Being a Lighthouse Professor in the University," in which he shares winsome and legal ways to self-identify as a Christian professor. The third talk addresses legal concerns many Christian professors have and includes five examples from his own career when he overcame challenges by the upper university administration to the legality of his Christian presence and activities. All five issues were resolved favorably through legal opinions provided by TAMU's legal office.

Two years after Walter's retirement from Baylor, in 2014, he and Ann moved to Sun City, a retirement community in Georgetown, Texas, and soon reached out to make friends with their new neighbors. Because the development sold lots one block at a time, everyone moved in around the same time. "It was like freshman year at college," Walter said. "Everyone was new. Everyone had left their old friends behind and was looking to make new ones." The Bradleys began hosting book studies and Bible studies, inviting Christian and non-Christian neighbors alike. One book they shared was John Burke's *Imagine Heaven*, which presents compelling empirical evidence that there is life after death and which sold 500,000 copies in its first two months. Burke had asked Dr. Bradley to review the book as a scientist, not a Christian, and Bradley's review was on page two. He had written that the book "masterfully combines the surprisingly large amount of empirical data from interviews with people who have near

Ann and Walter Bradley (2016)

death experiences (NDEs), usually in emergency rooms at hospitals, with data from the Scriptures to create a remarkably believable picture of what life after death will be like."

Hoping to get six couples to attend a discussion about *Imagine Heaven*, Ann and Walter invited twelve. To their amazement, all twelve came the first week and all but one continued for the whole six-week series. Before the series was finished, other people who heard about the discussions called to ask if the series would be repeated. Ann and Walter repeated their study for another set of neighbors. Based on what those neighbors told others, there was a demand for the Bradleys to host a third and fourth series. "It was a remarkable experience," Walter said, "unlike any study we had done in the past forty years."

Some participants wanted to continue to meet after the study was finished. That has led to an ongoing Bible study fellowship group of about sixteen neighbors who have become like extended family to each other, helping and praying for each other and enjoying rich fellowship and honest sharing every Sunday night in the Bradley home.

Walter has found another opportunity to serve in Georgetown by teaching two six-week-long classes each year at Georgetown Seniors University, an organization of about seven hundred seniors who are eager to keep learning. Walter's wide range of topics have included near-death experiences, movies that raise interesting questions about life, the origin of life, ten inventions that changed the world, and the Bible and science. Recently he was invited to join the curriculum committee in addition to teaching.

Not that teaching and the rest take up all of his time. He still occasionally plays golf and softball, goes to Pilates class and dancing with Ann, and walks ten thousand steps a day.

* * *

This account of Walter Bradley's life and career to date is as fully dimensional as possible, drawing on the subject himself as well as family, friends, colleagues, and our own personal experiences for information and insights. Walter will no doubt take issue with the finished product, insisting it puts him in a much better light than is truthful or than he deserves.

No responsible biographer wants to be accused of producing a hagiography, a one-sided account that covers only the admirable parts of a person's life and ignores or shortchanges the rest. Is it a hagiography, though, when the story is indeed a complete account but there simply isn't anything critical to report? Can Walter, always a modest and self-effacing man (except when giving expert testimony on the witness stand to a hostile lawyer), fairly criticize the effort as too laudatory, too complimentary?

Your authors, having done their due diligence, have found themselves at the mercy of the facts. Walter Bradley is an extraordinary husband, father, grandfather, Christian, engineer, scientist, colleague, friend, and mentor. He overcame tragic events early on that would have swamped the lives of less resilient and less resolute young people. He worked hard, treated others with fairness and compassion, and put his trust in God. He

Walter is also an occasional thespian. Here he is in full makeup as the apostle "doubting Thomas" in his church's 2019 Easter play.

has become successful by every measure, while remaining kind, humble, and as eager as ever to tackle the next interesting challenge down the road.

It is true that he loves to save a nickel and he's usually late. But he saves out of habit formed when he had little and was determined to pay his own way regardless.

We solicited testimonials about Walter Bradley that appear at the end of this book. One of the respondents, Professor Brian Thomas, addended his response with a tongue-in-cheek remark: "In the name of authenticity, I must reveal that he was always late to meetings."

Walter is late because there's always something else to interest him that needs doing.

"As I look back," Walter recalled recently with a laugh, "my life ended up being a whole lot more exciting than I ever imagined because God had

Ann and Walter are front and center with Walter's sister, Linda Bradley Gamble, behind. Ann and Walter's fiftieth wedding anniversary is celebrated by their children, grandchildren, and spouses.

all kinds of plans for me if I would listen. I don't think I got them all right, but I think I got some of them right. I look back and say if I'd just gone and done what I thought made sense to me, I would have had a much, much more pedestrian life.

"I'm a good testimony, I think, to what kind of adventure God wants to take us on and how we often shy away from trusting Him and just going for it. I'm sure when I see the video reruns of my life I'll be going, 'Oh, how did I miss that?! Ooh, that would have been so cool!' But I feel like I got a lot of the things God had in store."

Walter did not want a book about how great he is. *He wanted a book about how great God is and how following Him is the key to all happiness and success.* "I hope that the take-home on this will be an encouragement for people who are Christians but they just want to take the safe, simple, go-along-to-get-along theme for their lives that they may have come up with. Instead, I hope they'll say God probably has something far more exciting and far more fruitful planned for me, something that will give them a life full of meaning and purpose.

"I think the life Ann and I have lived is a wonderful example of the possibilities. Because it's not that we're great or we're talented or so forth. I think what God wants us to be is just faithful. If we'll be faithful, then He has exciting things for everybody to do. It's a question of whether we're willing to step out in faith.

"There's a book called *If You Want to Walk on Water, You've Got to Get Out of the Boat* by John Ortberg. It is a great title and a great book. It reminded me that I think like the disciples of Jesus who knew Him personally and still did stupid things. Jesus walks on the water, then He calls Peter to walk on the water. Notice how none of the other disciples get out of the boat. When Peter walks a little bit and then starts thinking about what he's doing, he says, 'Oh my gosh, I'm sinking!' Well, you're supposed to keep your eyes on Christ. Don't worry about the water.

"I think our lives are often like that. God calls us to get out of the boat and we're going, 'Oh no, I can't do that!' Just keep your eyes on Christ. Don't worry about the water."

Appendix 1: Testimonies

We contacted people whose lives have been impacted by Walter and Ann Bradley. You will recognize some discussed in the book.

Our initial goal was to collect a few lines from a few people. The response was overwhelming. Respondents often suggested more names. "Have you contacted so-and-so?" If we hadn't, we did.

More than one told us that a few lines were not enough to talk about Walter Bradley. They were right. Some submitted pages, and we had to whittle them down. Even so, a number of the testimonials to follow are long paragraphs.

Celebrate with us the enormous impact a single man can make in a lifetime. More importantly, read as an enlightenment of your potential to change your world from your current station in life.

Personal Ministry

"Walter Bradley and his wife, Ann, helped my husband, Blake, and me through the most beautiful and most painful journey in our lives. We suddenly and unexpectedly lost our firstborn daughter, Olive, in 2015 when she was just shy of five months old. The days ahead were dark, dark, dark. But you know how they say a pin drop of light in a dark, dark room is still stronger, and offers hope. That's exactly what he and another dear friend, Dr. Don Byker, did. Dr. Bradley cried with us, prayed for us walking in the thick of the pain, and helped us stand when all we could do is collapse. Walter was close to us then and remains one of our closest friends. I first met Dr. Bradley when I was a student at Baylor University. He took me under his wing and helped me learn how to succeed. I graduated with top GPA both in my masters and then on to my PhD. He taught me how to slow down while accomplishing much. Dr. Bradley was both my master advisor at Baylor University and served on my PhD committee at the University of Colorado. He has been an amazing mentor, helping me learn to write technically and training me to be a PI [Principle Investigator] on National Science Foundation Grants. He helped me launch my first start-up. We started a company together in 2009 that gave me foundation for my second start-up in 2013. We launched three products into the marketplace made of coconut shell powder and coconut husk fibers. Dr. Bradley has been like a grandfather to Blake and me. He is a man of integrity, character, and kindness. His brilliance lies beyond academics. It's in the way he treats others. The way he inspires others and the way he cares for others while holistically pointing to the love of God. He never talks about God in an offensive manner but in a way where others want to know more about Christ."

Elisa Teipel, PhD, co-founder,
chief development officer, Essentium Inc.

"Walter Bradley helped me through a dark period in my life. On August 23, 2004, at the age of twenty, I was involved in a life-changing auto accident in South Dakota. I swerved to avoid hitting a varmint and flipped an SUV. I broke the C2 vertebrae in my neck—the same vertebrae broken by Christopher (Superman) Reeve that left him a quadriplegic. A nurse witnessed the wreck and came to my rescue. She set my neck correctly, avoiding damage to my spinal cord therefore avoiding the fate of the paralyzed Christopher Reeve. I was airlifted to a hospital in Sioux Falls where I awoke with a Halo unit literally screwed into my skull to keep my head immobile. Activities I took for granted were no longer allowed. Riding in a car was dangerous because of bumps. The Halo didn't let me turn my head. I couldn't shower. Finally home in Texas after a long, careful drive, I was housebound and feeling low. One of my dad's close friends found out and decided to visit me weekly. The man was Dr. Walter Bradley. We talked about life, love, and Christ. I lived in McGregor, Texas, and

Dr. Bradley's journey from Baylor took about a half hour each way. He visited me consistently for many months, sometimes just to hear me vent. He bought me books and was dedicated to cultivating my young mind. Eventually I recovered. It's rare to gain a friend at your lowest point in life. Dr. Bradley was that friend. Dr. Bradley's visits weren't glamorous to the world or a career advancer. He was a successful full-time distinguished professor yet somehow found a few hours a week to bless me with unconditional love with no expectation of worldly gain. This is pure Christian altruism. This is Walter Bradley."

Joshua J. Marks, teacher, Waco High School, Waco, Texas

"I met Jesus Christ through Walter Bradley. More than his scientific brilliance or dynamic leadership, he and Ann's humble integrity and love drew me. I was a confused, skeptical, searching college student. I was angry; Walter was gentle. I was inconsistent and volatile; he was steady and patient and loving. He listened respectfully to my confused questioning. Ever the skilled teacher, he nudged me to discover answers for myself. One day I found myself bawling like a baby with Walter. I had hid my inner turmoil, but Walter's unrelenting love broke through my walls. Then, as I began my faltering steps toward Christ, Walter saw potential I couldn't see, and step by step he encouraged me to grow and lead. We see, in public, bright and gifted individuals. But what are they like in private? Walter and Ann opened their lives to me. I saw their struggles. I watched Walter forgive when denied promotion due to his outspoken faith. In them I saw and experienced the genuine, unconditional love of Jesus Christ. They humbly walk the talk. One day few will remember Walter's worldly achievements. But his legacy will continue through us, the lives God touched through him. May we honor Walter and our Lord by loving both the Truth and those we meet, as he does."

Dennis Hesselbarth, pastor, Evangelical Free Church of America

"I got to know Dr. Walter Bradley during my time as a student at the Colorado School of Mines. I did well in my studies, but by my junior year I was beginning to wonder what life was about. The events that led to my accepting Christ had much to do with the ministry of Campus Crusade

for Christ at CSM, which was started by Dr. Bradley. It was the love
for one another, joy, and purpose among the Christian students with
Crusade that attracted me strongly to Christ. I finally saw my need for
the Savior in my last semester of school and trusted in Christ in early
1972. I will always be indebted to Dr. Bradley for founding and leading the ministry of Crusade at CSM. As a professor with a zeal for the
gospel, the Lord used him greatly in my life, and in the lives of many
others. Seven years later, after grad school in engineering and working
for a mining company, I left my job, went to seminary, and then my wife
and I served as missionaries with the Evangelical Alliance Mission for
twenty-eight years, sixteen years in Taiwan, and then twelve years in
the US."

George K. McFal Jr., the Evangelical Alliance Mission (retired)

"Dr. Walter Bradley has been such a blessing in my life for over twenty
years. Every time we have met he has always encouraged me and lifted my
soul. I thank the good Lord for having this saint influence my walk with
Jesus."

Denis O. Lamoureux, DDS, PhD,
professor of science and religion, St. Joseph's College,
University of Alberta

Academia

"Walter Bradley is one of the most remarkable Christian scholars I've
ever known. His arrival at Baylor University not only had a powerful
effect on an already good School of Engineering, but it had a transfor-
mative impact on the entire university. Walter used all of the gifts at
his disposal to improve the lives and careers of all those around him.
His colleagues benefited from his intellectual verve, his great personality, his teaching popularity, and his networks of influence in the broader
academic communities of science and engineering. Students benefited
from his great teaching and lively faith. And all of us as his colleagues
were encouraged by his enormous capacity to integrate historic Christian
faith with cutting-edge scientific thinking. Walter and Ann have made a

huge difference around the world for the cause of Christ, and those who have known them have been emboldened to share faith and live it more humbly."

> Robert B. Sloan, DTh, president, Houston Baptist University;
> past president, Baylor University;
> founding dean, George W. Truett Theological Seminary

"I first crossed paths with Walter Bradley when we happened to see him on a TV show hosted by Hugh Ross. Walter was outstanding—strong arguments with clear presentation. He was a great witness. We watched until the end to see who this guy was and where he was from. Imagine our delight when we learned the speaker, Professor Walter Bradley, was the chair of mechanical engineering at Texas A&M. The next day I made my way to his office and have been a Bradley fan ever since. Walter is an outstanding example and role model for young faculty. He greatly improved engineering at both Texas A&M and Baylor. Walter is a great friend and colleague; he is indeed and in fact a distinguished professor and Christian."

> Marlan Scully, PhD, Distinguished Research Academician,
> Baylor University; Distinguished Professor,
> Texas A&M University; member, National Academy of Sciences

"I first met Walter Bradley at Cedar Campus in Northern Michigan in the summer of 1998. He was well known and warmly regarded by all, and in our few brief conversations I could see that he was, in effect, already an exemplary Christian academic statesman. Only three years later I found myself unexpectedly charged with recruiting distinguished professors who would lead not merely in teaching and research at Baylor University but who could exemplify a Christian worldview in so doing. One of the first people I called on was Walter, and in the providence of God he and Ann were led to join us. He has been an extraordinary model and faithful witness here, and I count it a gift of the Lord to have been his colleague."

> David Lyle Jeffrey, FRSC, Distinguished Senior Fellow,
> Baylor Institute for Studies in Religion, Waco, Texas

"In 1976, I was asked to read and comment on a manuscript critiquing origin of life theories written by Walter Bradley and a coauthor for possible publication. I had just joined the staff of Probe Ministries in Dallas, and this was my first assignment. I read and liked much of what I read but wondered how a book on the origin of life could be effective without more chemistry. Jon Buell, cofounder of Probe, said he was going to College Station where Bradley had just joined the faculty of mechanical engineering at Texas A&M. 'Come with me and you can ask him.' So I did. Bradley and coauthor Roger Olsen were both at the Bradley residence, as his wife, Ann, welcomed us in for the weekend. We discussed the book and my reservations about it. Both Bradley and Olsen said, 'You're the chemist, you write it.' And that's how I got involved with the manuscript that was eventually published as *The Mystery of Life's Origin*. Some have called it foundational to the intelligent design movement. More than forty years after that weekend, I offer this assessment. First, Walter Bradley is a gifted teacher, skilled at making thermodynamics understandable. A major contribution to *Mystery* shows the role of the investigator in prebiotic simulation experiments as that of supplying at least a portion of what Bradley called configurational entropy work that results in specific sequences of amino acids in proteins and nucleotides in nucleic acids (DNA and RNA) and in cell assembly. In my view that is a monumental achievement. In addition to numerous scholarly enterprises in which Walter has excelled, his personal life is exemplary and his counsel helpful. I am happy to call him my friend."

Charles B. Thaxton, PhD, Konos Connection,
Peachtree City, Georgia

Personal Mentoring

"I had the honor of working with Walter for six years while studying under him during graduate school at Baylor and helping him start our coconut composites business. He spent the end of his professional career pouring into the beginning of mine, and I am forever grateful for his example. He modeled for me how to be a professor and researcher while finding creative ways to minister to others using my gifts and interests. We became a source of mutual support during his and my late wife's cancer trials, and he remains a dear friend whose enduring lessons continue to grow my admiration of him."

Professor Stanton Greer,
Department of Mechanical Engineering, Baylor University

"Walter Bradley has directly mentored me in my scientific and religious life. For the past three decades, I have asked him countless questions about my future, and he has patiently answered them all and given me wise counsel. He and his wife, Ann, have also indirectly mentored me by providing living examples of what it means to be Christians who also happen to be involved in academia. To this day, when I sit down and talk with them, the stories they share about what they do, how they think, and how they feel shed light on the path in front of me and my wife. I am deeply indebted to them, as I know many other people are. They have had an enormous impact on my life."

Jed C. Macosko, PhD, professor of physics,
Wake Forest University

"Walter and his lovely bride, Ann, are an inspiration. Their influence on my life cannot be measured. The Lord put him in my life at the time I was most uncertain about both my personal and professional life. Walter has the unique talent of being able to simultaneously discuss the most technical and intricate of scientific challenges while viewing the larger impact of his work. I was continually amazed how every technical conversation I had with him always had a thread of the conversation that focused my personal development, both in my walk with the Lord and my family. He wanted to be sure that people were progressing professionally while understanding that we have a higher calling and the real prize was awaiting us in heaven. It is rare to find a couple with such a passion for the Lord."

David Jack, PhD, professor of mechanical engineering,
Baylor University

"I first met Walter Bradley a quarter century ago when he gave a talk on scientific evidence for God's existence at Northwestern University in

Evanston, Illinois, where I was doing my PhD in philosophy of physics. Not long after, we crossed paths again at a conference in California where he spoke on evidence for design in the mathematical form of physical laws and the fine-tuning of universal constants. His insights gave me a healthy appreciation of the limitations of physical systems and encouraged my research on the implications of quantum physics for the metaphysics of intelligent causation in nature. We later were colleagues for a short time at Baylor University. It was there I really saw Walter's heart for ministry in addition to his intellect. He humbly mentored other faculty—myself included—in matters of Christian scholarship. I watched as he and his wife, Ann, moved into campus residences to be spiritual and academic advisors to undergraduate students. The students were never in better hands than they were with the Bradleys. From his passion for advancing the intellectual claims of the gospel on university campuses around the country, to his privately mentoring students and faculty in the Christian faith, to his academic work and service, to his humanitarian engineering projects in third world countries, Walter is, by the grace and gifting of God, a force of nature. I count it an honor and a privilege to know him."

Bruce L. Gordon, PhD, associate professor of the history and philosophy of science, Houston Baptist University, Center for Science and Culture; Senior Fellow, Discovery Institute

"Walter Bradley helped guide me on my current course in life. I first met Dr. Bradley while pursuing a masters' degree at Baylor University. He quickly became a man I looked up to and sought guidance from. I still seek his advice. I appreciated his example of a life lived for Christ, unashamed of being counted with Him regardless of the worldly costs. He was able to make an impact in his research field, yet always put people, and particularly students, first. I've learned from his example, and have sought to emulate it in my own life. As an assistant professor beginning my academic career, I am inspired by Dr. Bradley in the way I interact with my own students, and in the vigor with which I pursue my research. Inviting students over to my home for meals, having Bible studies with believing and agnostic students alike, and giving my full strength to research excellence—these are all things I've learned from Dr. Bradley. I continue to learn from his faithfully lived life and his making an impact for Christ wherever he goes. Because of his investment in lives like mine, his impact will outlast his own life for many generations to come."

George D. Montañez, PhD, Iris and Howard Critchell
assistant professor, Department of Computer Science,
Harvey Mudd College

"Knowing and being mentored by Walter Bradley has been one of God's greatest blessings. Through his conference talks, time spent with Walter and Ann, and traveling on international ministry trips with him, I learned most of what I know about how Christian academics can leave an enduring legacy when they step away from the academy. Walter's examples of standing up for Christ in the university reminded me of what it really looks like when we seek to please our Lord above all else, since the prevalent culture is to bury our faith solely in private thoughts and church attendance. Walter and Ann's wise counsel was invaluable when my wife and I were praying about taking early retirement in order to join the staff of Faculty Commons, Cru's faculty ministry. To have Walter as a dear brother in Christ and mentor for over thirty years will always be a highlight of my Christian walk."

John F. Walkup, PhD, Emeritus Horn Professor of
Electrical and Computer Engineering,
Texas Tech University (1971–1998); staff member,
Faculty Commons/Cru; San Francisco Bay Area campuses (1998–2020)

"My wife knew whenever I met with Walter Bradley a new book would arrive a few days later. You see, Walter shared my enthusiasm for talking, reading, and studying God, and I naturally gravitated toward him for discipleship. I became a follower of Jesus Christ in 2010 when I was a postdoctoral researcher in mathematics at Baylor University. As a result, I desperately wanted to learn how to be a professor on a mission, a so-called Christian professor. When I took my first academic position at a secular university, Walter guided me through a ready supply of excellent discipleship books, many of which I have used in helping others come to know who Jesus is. During that first year as an assistant professor, Walter and

I met regularly through Skype, discussing books, the Bible, and life as a professor. His commitment to me provided enrichment to my spiritual growth and maturing into the professor I am now. Moreover, Walter intentionally chose studies and books that augmented my mission as a Christian professor and aided my efforts in sharing my faith with my students and colleagues. Walter would share numerous comical stories from his early years as a professor, which provided me with tremendous encouragement to be bold and genuine about my faith in Jesus. To this day, I thank God for his mentorship and for providing me a model to imitate, just as Paul suggested in 1 Corinthians 11:1."

Matthew Beauregard, PhD, professor of mathematics,
Stephen F. Austin State University

"I first met Walter when he visited our campus in the early 1980s to encourage us to form a Christian faculty network. We quickly connected through our mutual research interests and love for Jesus. We did form CFN, which continues today, and Walter became my mentor. He invited me to be his roommate at a summer research conference. I loved his Origins talk and used his *Mysteries of Life's Origins* book to develop my own lecture on the origin of the first cells. This grew into a seminar course on *Origins* at Minnesota, which received a Templeton Foundation award. Walter gave guest lectures in the course even when I taught with my son Jed at Berkeley. Walter invited me to attend Cru conferences where my wife, Kathleen, and Ann became fast friends. We have skied together, visited each other's homes, and continue to work on projects and pray together. I have been blessed by our friendship for over thirty years."

Chris Macosko, PhD, Professor Emeritus, chemical engineering
and materials science, University of Minnesota

University Campus Ministry

"Professor Walter Bradley fearlessly led the charge for faculty to unabashedly stand up for their faith on campuses. He was a tremendous example to me personally throughout the 1990s and 2000s, where he partnered with college campus ministries to strengthen and unite faculty around the country.

It is much harder to get faculty to step forward in defense of their faith than it is to get students to stand up. Professor Bradley taught us how it's done."

James M. Tour, PhD, T. T. and W. F. Chao professor of chemistry,
Rice University

"My respect and admiration for Walter Bradley has continued to grow since the first time I met him three decades ago. I've been privileged to observe how he presents scientific evidences for the truth of the Bible and the Christian gospel to both students and peers, including colleagues at the highest academic levels. He does so boldly, based on in-depth research, and always in a gracious, compassionate manner. He approaches audiences, whether friendly or otherwise, with gentleness, kindness, patience, love, and humility. One of the great blessings God has granted me in my life is the opportunity to have co-ministered with him among faculty and students on university campuses across the United States and beyond. Walter's ingenuity and integrity as a scientist and his humble character as a follower of Christ make him a worthy example to all. May we honor and bless him by diligently developing sound reasons for our faith and confidently presenting those reasons with gentleness, respect, and a clear conscience whenever and wherever God leads."

Hugh Ross, PhD, Reasons to Believe

"Dr. Bradley has not only impacted the national conversation on science and theism, he has also left an amazing legacy from his years at Texas A&M and Baylor. In the 1980s, Dr. Bradley was instrumental in the formation and growth of a Christian Faculty Network at Texas A&M. This organization has allowed for countless conversations about eternal matters between faculty, staff, and students. Texas A&M's unique culture stems from faculty who deeply care about character formation for our students, and Dr. Bradley's welcoming, thoughtful, creative approach to engaging students is a hallmark of that culture. Even today among the faculty, Dr. Bradley's name carries tremendous weight because we know what an impact and legacy that he has left us."

Micah Green, PhD, professor of chemical engineering,
Texas A&M; Texas A&M Christian Faculty Network

"Walter Bradley has been an inspiration to a great many Christians in the academic world. Without Walter's example, many Christian academics would have barricaded their lives in Christ from their scholarly research."

Dr. Henry F. Schaefer III, PhD, professor of chemistry, Graham Perdue; director, Center for Computational Quantum Chemistry, University of Georgia

"In his humble, quietly courageous manner Walter Bradley has faithfully pioneered the way for Christ-following professors for six decades. This is an incalculably great gift to the world, as our broken world desperately needs the unique contributions of scholars who are shaped by Christ. For years to come Christian academics will look to him in admiration and gratitude, finding in his life story the encouragement and wisdom to boldly follow Christ into the wonderful world of academe. Words seem insufficient to express our gratitude, both to God and to Walter, for the impact of this life so well lived."

Rick Hove, national director, Faculty Commons, the faculty ministry of Cru

"Long ago I learned that Walter Bradley has a commanding stage presence. In 1992, a conference was held at Southern Methodist University to celebrate the publication of Phillip Johnson's book *Darwin on Trial*. Near the end of it, a number of us lesser participants were invited to share the stage with Phil and Michael Ruse in a public Q&A session. During the session, I wanted to make a point, but the two headliners were dominating the conversation and the microphone. I turned to Walter, who was the session moderator, and asked sotto voce if I could speak next. When Michael Ruse finished his point and Phil Johnson made a grab for the microphone, Walter told him in no uncertain terms that I was next to speak. Even Phil Johnson did what Walter Bradley told him to do!"

Michael J. Behe, PhD, professor of biochemistry, Lehigh University

"There are few men who have had more impact on Christian ministry than Dr. Walter Bradley. He, along with my mentor, Prof. Rae Mellichamp, founded the Faculty Ministry of Cru in the late 1970s. Through Rae, I met Dr. Bradley almost thirty-five years ago. I have heard him speak in his West Texas drawl scores of times, and I never tire of hearing his adventures in Christian ministry in higher education. He admits his fears in campus ministry. His willingness to overcome his fears for the sake of Jesus Christ is inspirational. He demonstrated integration of his Christian faith with his academic knowledge in his co-authoring in 1984, *The Mystery of Life's Origin*. Dr. Bradley is a true pioneer in the area of Christian ministry on the college and university campus. His influence on Christian ministry by professors continues to impact thousands of lives. To paraphrase Isaac Newton, 'If we have seen further in ministry to Christian professors, it is because we stand on the shoulders of giants like Dr. Bradley.'"

Phil Bishop, PhD, Emeritus Professor, exercise science,
University of Alabama; affiliate staff,
Cru Faculty Commons Ministry

"I was introduced to Dr. Bradley while a university student hearing his 'Scientific Evidence for God' talk. Years later, as a full-time ministry worker on the University of Washington campus, I brought in Dr. Bradley to speak to students and faculty on issues related to intelligent design. Hundreds attended and lives were deeply impacted to various degrees as a result, including the launching of a faculty ministry at the University of Washington. I am deeply indebted to his scholarship and commitment to influencing the modern university."

Brian Ricci, national field director,
Bridges International (a ministry of Cru)

"Walter has been a close personal friend and colleague since we first met in the 1970s as engineering professors at Texas A&M University. He has been an inspiration to me both as a brother in Christ and academician. I have found his arguments for the existence of a divine creator based on scientific evidence to be very convincing, and helpful to me in strengthening my faith and witnessing for Christ."

Richard Schapery, PhD, Professor Emeritus,
Cockrell Family Regents Chair; emeritus in engineering,
the University of Texas at Austin

Appropriate Technology for Developing Countries

"Walter was instrumental in helping me to understand that my gifts and talents as an engineer could be used to serve the poor and marginalized, both at home and abroad. This has helped me go to the next level in my faith journey; now my engineering design work seems like worship. He encouraged me to form a student organization called Engineers with a Mission at Baylor University that collaborates on engineering projects in poor countries. In fact, I am writing this from Haiti as I work on solar energy systems for the medical community here. Thank you, Walter, for helping me find my vocation."

Professor Brian Thomas, senior lecturer of electrical
and computer engineering, Baylor University;
executive director, Justice and Mercy Energy Services

"Dr. Bradley visited Petra Christian University in Indonesia where I worked. He shared his vision of helping us, a private university, to understand the integration of science and Christian faith by using appropriate technology. He showed us not everything our country threw away was waste. Dr. Bradley envisioned turning worthless coconut husk into a product of value. It was an honor and a privilege for me to accompany him to places on many of Indonesia's islands. During our short period of traveling together, Dr. Bradley shared his life and told me of his terminal illness. I learned from Dr. Bradley important life lessons and spiritual aspects that have allowed him to have a strong, fruitful life. Dr. Bradley then opened a way for me to attend Baylor University in Waco, Texas. I am grateful for his continuing influence on the world and in my life for his engineering genius and his dedication to Christ."

Iwan Njoto Sandjaja, lecturer, Petra Christian University, Indonesia

"When I was a PhD student in 1994 at Texas A&M, Walter Bradley learned that I was a Christian who came to know the Lord during the time when early Baptist missionaries came to Papua New Guinea early in the 1940s. (My father was one of these early converts who worked with missionaries. God revealed to my father in a dream I was to be named Yuhanan. But the early Australian missionary nurses advised my dad that the name Yuhanan means John in English and they advised my dad to name me John, and he did.) Frequently, Walter and I would get together during lunch hours to pray and share matters of interest about God. Walter was on my PhD committee. Later in 2004, when Walter was at Baylor, he invited me to be a research professor to work on a project using virgin coconut oil to produce coconut biodiesel as an alternative fuel for diesel engines. The project was a success and is currently being used in a number of coconut-producing countries in the Pacific Islands. This project was initiated by Walter because he wanted to assist small countries like mine to improve the people's living standards. During these times, we would get together regularly to have fellowship and pray and share about God and our relationship with Him. I thank God for making it possible for me to meet Walter as my mentor in my studies, research, and a prayer warrior colleague."

Professor John Pumwa, PhD, head of department and acting dean of engineering, Mechanical Engineering Department, PNG University of Technology, Papua New Guinea

Inspiration

"Walter Bradley woke me from my dogmatic slumber. As a Christian college student, I had tried to reconcile my religious beliefs with what I took to be the best origin-of-life science. Walter's work convinced me that materialistic origin-of-life theories fell flat, and that intelligent design fit the facts much better. That change of mind permanently altered my career trajectory, and for that, I'll always be grateful."

Jay W. Richards, PhD, research assistant professor, the Busch School of Business, the Catholic University of America

"Walter Bradley is one of the most extraordinary men I have ever known. I am in awe of him. I have never seen anyone with a bigger heart for people. He and his wife, Ann, have given of their lives freely and sacrificially to university students, opening their home and ministering to them. It staggers the imagination how a busy professor, pursuing a scholarly career and pulling in millions of dollars in research grants to the university, could have the time and energy to carry out what is effectively the full-time duties of a campus minister. He is truly amazing!"

William Lane Craig, PhD, DTheol,
Talbot School of Theology, ReasonableFaith.org

"Luminaries like Walter Bradley paved the way for me to dedicate my career to advancing design thinking in biology. And when my career was thrown into turmoil because of that decision, Walter was there to help—with his broad smile, his inexhaustible wisdom, and his natural way of putting his influence to good use. Gracious to the core, he's one of a few people I mentally summon when I find myself in a situation that requires unnatural calm."

Douglas Axe, PhD, Maxwell Professor of molecular biology,
Biola University; Author of *Undeniable:*
How Biology Confirms Our Intuition That Life Is Designed

"I first met Walter Bradley in 1991 in Leningrad, Russia. He was there speaking at the university, not only sharing his scientific expertise, but also his Christian faith. I was so impressed with this brilliant professor so bold about his faith. Nearly three decades later, I invited Dr. Bradley to speak at a citywide event called Explore God. To my excitement, Dr. Bradley started coming to our church after moving to Austin and immediately plugged in teaching and leading outreaches in his community. Walter is the most humble, smart, godly, initiative-taking, bold leader that I know. He's made a huge impact on earth, for the scholarly and the poor, and great will be his reward in heaven."

John Burke, founder and lead pastor, Gateway Church,
Austin, Texas; author of *Imagine Heaven:*
Near-Death Experiences, God's Promises,
and the Exhilarating Future That Awaits You

"Dr. Walter Bradley was one of my teachers and my advisor when I studied for my PhD at Colorado School of Mines, Golden, Colorado. A strong friendship was born from that interaction, and has been growing for fifty years! During our period in Golden, Walter and his loving wife, Ann, blessed me and my family with their Christian love, helping us through some difficult times. Walter and family later spent time in Brazil as visiting professor at my university, the Federal University of Minas Gerais. Later I had a two-year period as visiting professor at Texas A&M University, where he was a full professor. Dr. Bradley is a top teacher, full of enthusiasm and competence, and a world-class researcher in the area of Materials Science. I am always amazed at his capacity of 'creating time' to be so effective and brilliant in both areas.

"Living the Christian faith, he always demonstrates love and concern for those with whom he interacts."

Carlos Bottrel Coutinho, PhD, Professor Emeritus,
Federal University of Minas Gerais, Brazil

"Walter Bradley was my professor at Texas A&M. It is his example that still guides me today as a faculty member and parent in setting God, family, and career as the order of priorities."

Nandika D'Souza, PhD, professor and associate dean,
University of North Texas

"Walter Bradley has been a friend, advisor, and source of inspiration for me and the Hill Country Institute from the beginning of the institute's efforts to serve the body of Christ. Walter's collegial and respectful way of interacting with Christians who share a deep commitment to Jesus Christ, but who disagree on aspects of faith and science, opened doors for us to build trust and bring leaders together from a variety of perspectives. Walter is truly a statesman in a day and age when statesmanship is a welcome breath of fresh air. Walter and Ann have graciously been available to assist in encouraging and equipping the body of Christ by sharing their insight and wisdom from many years of integrating faith, life, and scholarship. They are exemplars of living the words of C. S. Lewis, 'We should be like a bird with two wings, developing our faith and our career.' We are thankful for Walter and Ann's generosity, thoughtfulness, leadership, and kindness. Knowing them is a blessing."

Larry Linenschmidt, executive director, Hill Country Institute;
host, Hill Country Institute Live: Exploring Christ & Culture

"I have known Walter Bradley for over ten years. My life has been truly enriched in knowing such a kind and warmhearted man. He inspires us to always have faith in God because the Lord gives us strength to accept life's challenges. I am so proud to be in his company of friends. Dr. Bradley has been an amazing blessing to me."

Minnie Simcik, graduate program coordinator, Baylor University

"Walter and I first met when I was new assistant professor in the business school at Texas A&M University in 1984. I learned from Walter that you can live out loud as a Christian academic. By his faith and academic credentials, he testifies to the compatibility of faith and science. Over the years, I saw him boldly confront high-level campus administrators, surprisingly some Christians, who occasionally wanted to deny Christian faculty their constitutional rights of freedom of religious expression and freedom of speech, mostly out of a desire to be politically correct. Being outnumbered or outranked never dismayed him from boldly speaking the truth. He helped start Christian Faculty Network and was its leader for many years. Walter said professors should work hard and strive to make significant academic contributions, but not at all costs. Keep God and family first. He said that if making tenure requires you to give all your time to work, it's not worth it. That advice served me well in the years to come. Professors can 'lose their lives' pursuing publications. He inspired and mentored many faculty members, including me."

Dr. Lawrence Murphy Smith, CPA, professor of accounting,
College of Business, RELLIS Campus,
Texas A&M University-Corpus Christi

"About fifteen years ago, I was going through some books found at my church library when I stumbled upon one entitled *The Mystery of Life's Origin* by Charles B. Thaxton, Walter L. Bradley, and Roger L. Olsen. I was surprised to find a book title like this among the Bibles, theology textbooks, and commentaries. I was immediately captured by the topic and the technical nature of the book. The book addressed concisely and with great clarity problems I thought faced the conventional picture of life's origins but had gone far beyond. The upshot of the book is that chemical and physical laws alone cannot explain life's origins—a very unwelcomed view in the contemporary debate concerning life's origins. I could not put the book down—its impact would change my life forever and helped me to redefine my career. Several years passed and I wondered if I could contact the authors. I learned that Dr. Bradley was a retired faculty member of Baylor and emailed him. After some exchanges, I was soon invited to Baylor by Dr. Bradley. When I met him at the airport he warmly greeted me as though I had known him for years. He swept up my bag, put it into his car trunk, and off we went. When we arrived at his house, he and Ann treated me like a family member! I also remembered thinking that if this is a retired man, what did the non-retired Walter Bradley look like? I have met only a handful of truly gracious, kindly, and openly godly men, gifted with intellectual abilities and the skill to express it. Dr. Bradley is surely among them. I will always treasure Dr. Bradley and that life-changing book upon that dusty old shelf. I now know that it was in just the right place."

John M. DeMassa, PhD, MDiv, Vanderbilt Chemicals, LLC;
lecturer, Housatonic Community College

"The career—which is to say, ministry—I have been in for the past thirty-plus years was profoundly shaped by Walter Bradley. It is not an overstatement to say that the way God used Walter and his ministry and testimony in my life is the primary motivation for why and how I ended up as a college professor. Before I ever had a chance to meet him, I heard about the work he was doing, and God used that to give me a vision and sense of calling that led me to graduate school, and once in graduate school to have a commitment to ministry. In graduate school at Cornell, I had a couple of opportunities to meet Walter in person and interact with him, and those personal interactions—hearing more of his testimony and stories, coming from a grace-filled, passionate heart—solidified all that I had previously heard and helped inspire me to keep going."

Matthew Dickerson, professor of computer science,
Middlebury College, Vermont

"The more you know Walter and Ann Bradley, the more you are amazed. Few know, for example, Walter and Ann were instrumental in the founding of one of our nation's first crisis pregnancy centers when Walter was a professor at Texas A&M. When Walter recruited my husband, Bob, to come to Baylor in 2003, we had a competing offer for another endowed chair position. I asked Bob if there was anyone he admired more and would want to work with than Walter Bradley. The answer made clear where we would move. And I would have more time with my remarkable friend Ann."

Monika Marks, McGregor, Texas

"At a 1970 meeting at Campus Crusade headquarters, Walter Bradley challenged my wife, Peggy, and me to join Crusade as associate staff members, which we did, serving in that capacity until joining full-time in 1994 at my retirement from the university. We became close friends, and Walter and I were invited to be frequent conference speakers in what became to be known as 'the Rae and Roy' show—Roy being a sobriquet for Walter who looked a bit like Roy Rogers, the famous cowboy. The Bradleys and the Mellichamps traveled together with several other professors and staff on Christian Leadership Ministries' first international trip to South Africa in 1984. What a trip that was. Walter and I resurrected the Rae and Roy show in Johannesburg, and the videos were used in Capetown and other locations in South Africa. Over the years we have traveled with Walter and Ann to many locations, always sharing the things the Lord had been teaching us about ministering in the secular university. We were together in St. Petersburg (Leningrad at the time) and Kosovo. Peggy and Ann had key roles in the women's ministry, both working to develop outreach strategies and materials for women in academia and speaking many times here in the United States and internationally as well. Walter and Ann have been true soul mates for nearly fifty years. It is not an overstatement to say that had the Mellichamps not met the Bradleys at that conference in 1970 and been challenged by Walter to 'come help change the world' as associate staff, we would not have had the long-term relationship with Faculty Commons and Cru that we were blessed to have. Thanks, Walter and Ann! We love you and look forward to spending eternity together with you in the place Jesus has prepared for us. Hope our mansion is close to yours!"

Joseph McRae Mellichamp PhD, Emeritus Professor of management science, the University of Alabama

"Thanks to Dr. Bradley's work, we have reason to believe that scientific naturalism is not the best explanation for the way things are. Life cannot arise from non-life simply by chance, and there is an apparent design in nature that seems to demand a transcendent intelligence, an intelligence that many would recognize as 'God.' This has been a huge encouragement for Christian students who found their faith put on trial by the academic community, myself included. But Walter Bradley is much more than just a great scientist. He is a humanitarian, a man willing to give his time and resources to serve those in need both domestically and abroad, often in the face of strong adversity. As a professor, he has been his students' foremost advocate and an incredible mentor. As an ambassador for Christ, he is unwavering; he has committed his life to displaying God's truth and love to the world. I have witnessed his resolve and generosity firsthand, his willingness to give of himself without asking anything in return, and there is no doubt that he is a man worth emulating."

Ryan Crews, board of directors, CrossExamined.org

"I was surprised when God called me to academia. I had no idea what it meant to be a professor. I stumbled upon Dr. Walter Bradley in a Campus Crusade for Christ publication and cold-called him to ask for advice on transitioning from being an undergraduate mechanical engineering student to becoming a university professor. In 1993, I entered the PhD program at Texas A&M, with Dr. Bradley as my advisor. Over four years, and countless hours, Walter mentored me in proposal writing, publishing, research, and living as a Christian academic, husband, and father. Psalm 127:4 says, "Like arrows in the hands of a warrior are the sons born in one's youth." In many ways I feel like this verse applies to Walter. He is an academic warrior. His grad student 'children' have been sent like arrows to change the world. Throughout my eighteen years in academia and subsequent years in industry, Walter continues to be an inspiration for how to live a life of excellence in my career and as a child of God."

Brent Stucker, PhD, director, Additive Manufacturing, ANSYS, Inc.

"Being the quintessential gentleman, Walter Bradley is a treasure to befriend. He excels in civility and is always ready to engage in passionate but respectful dialog. It is a privilege to have counted him as a good friend for fifteen years and to have known and read his work for an additional fifteen years. While we have differed on many nuances, we share a deep faith in Christ and a commitment to integrity in science that is only strengthened by our ongoing conversation. We have grown in respect for each other as we seek to understand our respective ideas."

Randy Isaac, PhD, IBM Research VP of Science and Technology (retired); executive director emeritus, American Scientific Affiliation

"Early in his career as a professor, Walter Bradley began to influence my life and ministry as a young Cru staff member. In his seven years as an undergrad and grad student, Walter had not had a professor that he knew to be a Christian, and he was determined to make sure his students knew at least one. For his own students and countless thousands of others worldwide, Walter became that one professor. For over forty years, and as a founding professor of Cru's Faculty Commons, his mission has also been to help other Christian faculty do the same. By his joyful and kind demeanor Walter displays how Christianity is lived, and by his lectures and discussions on faith-science issues he shows why Christianity is true. For so many of us who have been greatly strengthened and encouraged by him, and who have seen secular scholarship and biblical faith united by him, Walter is the embodiment of 'that one professor.'"

Rich McGee, director of Ministry Development, Faculty Commons

"'Finally, the most interesting thing that I would like for you to know about me is that I am a follower of Jesus Christ. And by that I do not mean that I just go to church. It is the very foundation of everything that I do, and I hope that you will see that it makes a difference in how I treat you this semester.' This is how Dr. Bradley concluded his introduction on the first day of class to countless students through the years. And he has taught thousands of other Christian professors to look for ways to winsomely shine their own lights for Christ by speaking at hundreds of Christian faculty conferences over the years. What a difference he has made!"

Bonnie McGee, director of Conferences, Faculty Commons

"Walter has a well-trained academic mind together with a heart for others that leads him to think outside the box to solve real-world problems. His humble manner combined with authenticity make him a leader that others naturally want to follow. He and his wife, Ann, were very encouraging to us in the early days of establishing a ministry to faculty members and grad students at the University of Washington."

Ken and Francie Knutzen, Director Emeritus, Arbor Ministries

"Walter Bradley is unique as a professor, champion of ministries, and valued friend. Few Christian scholars have embraced their calling to the academy in such a powerful way. Walter created a model for colleagues in the way he excelled in scholarship, integrated his faith into his academics, and proclaimed his faith in a natural way that flowed from who he is as a person. His initiative with faculty and graduate students at Texas A&M transformed the model of Christian graduate student communities across the country. His legacy will continue through future generations of scholars because of those he has mentored and those of us he befriended on our personal journey."

Nick Repak, President Emeritus, Grad Resources

Appendix 2: Campuses and Countries

B elow is a list, though incomplete, of more than one hundred universities in the United States where Walter Bradley ministered, including those where he presented his lecture "Scientific Evidence for the Existence of God." He visited many of these universities more than once.

Amherst College
Arizona State University
Baylor University
Brown University
Cal Polytechnic University San
    Luis Obispo
Case Western University
Clemson University
Colorado School of Mines
Colorado State University
Cornell University
Dartmouth College
Florida State University
Georgia Tech
Gordon Conwell College
Illinois State University
Indiana University
Iowa State University
Kansas State University
Letourneau University

Louisiana State University
Louisiana Tech
Massachusetts Institute of
    Technology
Michigan State University
Middle Tennessee State University
Middlebury College
Mississippi State University
Montana State University
Northwestern University
Ohio State University
Ohio University
Oklahoma State University
Oral Roberts University
Oregon State University
Penn State University
Portland State University
Purdue University
Smith College
Southern Methodist University

Stanford University
Texas A&M University
Texas A&M University at
    Kingsville
Texas A&M University at
    Prairie View
Texas Christian University
Texas Tech University
University of Alabama
University of Arizona
University of Arkansas
University of California Berkeley
University of California
    Los Angeles
University of California
    San Diego
University of Colorado
University of Delaware
University of Florida
University of Georgia
University of Houston
University of Idaho
University of Illinois
University of Kansas
University of Kentucky
University of Maine
University of Maryland
University of Massachusetts
University of Michigan
University of Minnesota
University of Mississippi

University of Missouri at Columbia
University of Missouri at Rolla
University of Montana
University of New Mexico
University of North Dakota
University of Northern Colorado
University of Oklahoma
University of Oregon
University of Pennsylvania
University of Rhode Island
University of South Carolina
University of Southern California
University of Tennessee
University of Texas
University of Texas Arlington
University of Texas Austin
University of Texas El Paso
University of Texas San Antonio
University of Utah
University of Virginia
University of Washington
    Bellingham
University of Washington Seattle
University of Wisconsin
University of Wisconsin Lacrosse
University of Wyoming
Utah State University
Virginia Tech
Washington State University
Wheaton University
Williams College

Walter also lectured internationally on science and faith in the following countries:

Brazil	India	Russia
Canada	Italy	South Africa
China	Japan	South Korea
England	Kenya	Sweden
France	Kosovo	Switzerland
Germany	Mexico	
Greece	Peru	

Citations

Chapter 1

Information for this chapter is intermingled from three sources:

"The 'Progress' of a Faculty Pilgrim" by Walter L. Bradley, published in Rick Hove and Heather Holleman, eds., *A Grander Story: An Invitation to Christian Professors* (Orlando: CRU Press, 2017); Bradley interviews with author, Austin, Texas, May 7–10, 2018; and Bradley phone interview with author, October 18, 2018.

Chapter 2

Historical background on Corpus Christi taken from www.visitcorpurchristitx.org/trip -ideas/history; www.cctexas.com/departments/city-secretary/history-corpus-christi; and en.wikipedia.org/wiki/History_of_Corpus_Christi,_Texas.

Background on Dr. Bradley's early years is from email exchanges and phone calls with childhood friends Bill Lucas, Jerry Rodgers, Bob Brooks, Ray Goforth, JoAnn Goforth, and Nancy Moffett; and from conversations and correspondence with Dr. Bradley.

Information on the death of Kenneth Bradley and its aftermath is taken from interviews and from local newspaper coverage: "Local Father Kills Son, 18, Himself: Both Are Shot Through Head," *Corpus Christi Times*, August 4, 1958, 1.

Information about the University of Texas tower shooting taken from behindthetower. org; Texas State Historical Association at tshaonline.org/handbook/online/articles /jbu0; and contemporary TV coverage archived at www.youtube.com/watch?v=bBtrFS -C1ug.

Chapter 3

Specific details of Dr. Bradley's job search and hiring by Colorado School of Mines from email dated January 26, 2019. Further details from "The 'Progress' of a Faculty Pilgrim."

New Folk description from May 1968 concert audio posted on YouTube at www .youtube.com/watch?v=rMehWPDJR78, and The New Folk—Uprising! Review at www.discogs.com/The-New-Folk-Uprising/release/8225348.

Other specifics in this chapter taken from Dr. Bradley's email dated January 15, 2019, and interview on September 18–20, 2019.

Chapter 4

Information about Explo '72 taken from Dr. Bradley's interviews; "What Really Happened at Explo '72," www.cru.org/us/en/about/what-we-do/what-really-happened -at-explo-72; and en.wikipedia.org/wiki/Explo_'72.

Rich Wilson stories taken from Rich's phone interview, October 15, 2018.

Brazil trip details from interviews with Dr. Bradley.

Chapter 5

Information about perspectives of the Christian scholar from Dr. Bradley's chapter, "On Being a Christian Professor in the Secular Academy," in William Lane Craig and Paul M. Gould, eds., *The Two Tasks of the Christian Scholar: Redeeming the Soul Redeeming the Mind* (Wheaton, IL: Crossway Books, 2007).

Details of the family's move from Colorado to Texas are taken from various interviews and emails from Dr. Bradley to author; "A Grander Story"; phone interview with Dr. Steve Bradley on October 15, 2018; and interview with Sharon Bradley Perry, May 10, 2018.

The referenced papers are W. L. Bradley, W. J. Cantwell, and H. H. Kausch, "Viscoelastic Creep Crack Growth: A Review of Fracture Mechanical Analyses," *Mechanics of Time-Dependent Materials*, vol. 1 (1998), 241–68, and W. L. Bradley and M. N. Srinivasan, "Fracture and Fracture Toughness of Cast Irons," *International Materials Reviews*, vol. 35 (1990), 129, 162.

News features about upcoming innovations in the automotive industry are taken from the *Wall Street Journal*:

"Business Briefs," March 24, 1977, 1.

"Average Car to Weigh 700 Pounds Less by '85, Inland Steel Predicts," May 25, 1977, 33.

"Ford Enlarges Plans for Plant Expansion," August 30, 1977, 7.

"Business Briefs," September 15, 1977, 1.

Additional information about Campus Crusade for Christ at Texas A&M from interview with Katherine "Katy" Smith, April 5, 2018.

Balance of chapter about Air Force contract, expert witness testimony, run-ins with Texas A&M administration, and crisis pregnancy center all from interviews with Dr. Bradley on May 7–10, 2018, September 18–20, 2019, and related phone calls and emails. Additional details and background on lawsuits from interview with Dr. Steve Bradley, October 15, 2018.

Chapter 6

Information in this chapter taken from interviews and from the book Dr. Bradley spearheaded: Charles B. Thaxton, Walter L. Bradley, and Roger L. Olsen, *The Mystery of Life's Origin: Reassessing Current Theories* (New York: Philosophical Library, 1984).

Dr. Bradley recorded two interviews with this book's co-author, Robert J. Marks, about the writing of the original version of *The Mystery of Life's Origin*.

- Walter Bradley on the Newly Expanded Mystery of Life's Origin, January 29, 2020, https://www.discovery.org/multimedia/audio/2020/01/walter-bradley-on -the-newly-expanded-mystery-of-lifes-origin/.

- Walter Bradley on the New Mystery of Life's Origin, Part 2, February 5, 2020, https://www.discovery.org/multimedia/audio/2020/02/walter-bradley-on-the -new-mystery-of-lifes-origin-pt-2/.

Additional facts and supporting materials are from Dr. Bradley's chapter, "Does Recent Scientific Evidence Support an Intelligently Designed Universe?" in Paul Copan, Scott B. Luley, and Stan W. Wallace, eds., *Science: Christian Perspectives for the New Millennium* (Atlanta: RZIM, 1999); "Objection #3: Evolution Explains Life, So God Isn't Needed" in Lee Strobel, *The Case for Faith: A Journalist Investigates the Toughest Objections to Christianity* (Grand Rapids: Zondervan, 2000); and "Why I Believe the Bible Is Scientifically Reliable" in Norman L. Geisler and Paul K. Hoffman, eds., *Why I Am a Christian: Leading Thinkers Explain Why They Believe* (Grand Rapids: Zondervan, 2001).

Chapter 7

Details about Dr. Bradley's life and career are from interviews. Additional information about pizza nights and other outreach from "On Being a Christian Professor in the

Secular Academy," and "Ministering in the Postmodern Academy" in D. A. Carson, ed., *Telling the Truth: Evangelizing Postmoderns* (Grand Rapids: Zondervan, 2000).

Details of Steve's pursuit of a new car and Steve's reflections on growing up in the family are from cited interviews with Drs. Walter and Steve Bradley.

Chapter 8

The bulk of information in this chapter is from interviews and correspondence with Dr. Bradley. Additional details from interview with Dr. Steve Bradley.

Success4Students workbook and video published by Success4Students, 2002.

Information about Dr. Bradley's speaking itinerary is from David Klinghoffer's introduction to the reissue of *The Mystery of Life's Origin*.

Chapter 9

The bulk of information in this chapter is from interviews and correspondence with Dr. Bradley.

Science Speaks presentation information taken from Science Speaks DVD, January 2003, Orlando, Florida.

Chapter 10

Quotes and background from Dr. John Pumwa taken from email, October 11, 2018, and related correspondence.

Quotes from Elisa Teipel from email, June 26, 2019, and related correspondence and conversations.

For more on the Baylor Global Poverty Center see "Baylor Global Poverty Center – Executive Summary" at www.baylor.edu/content/services/document.php/39895.pdf.

Further information on the Global Poverty Center and Baylor 2012 from email and interview with Professor Brian Thomas, October 26, 2018.

Chapter 11

The bulk of information in this chapter is from interviews and correspondence with Dr. Bradley.

Quotes from "Why He Is a Hero: The Exemplary Life and Legacy of Dr. Walter Bradley," Robert J. Marks, https://centerforintelligence.org/about/walter-bradley/.

Quotes from "Launch of the Walter Bradley Center for Natural and Artificial Intelligence," July 12, 2018, https://billdembski.com/science-and-technology/launch-of -the-walter-bradley-center-for-natural-and-artificial-intelligence/.

Chapter 12

Information in this chapter is from interviews with Dr. Bradley, May 7–10, 2018, and September 18–20, 2019, and related correspondence and conversations.

John Burke, *Imagine Heaven: Near-Death Experiences, God's Promises, and the Exhilarating Future That Awaits You* (Grand Rapids: Baker Books, 2015).

Dr. Bradley discusses Burke's *Imagine Heaven* in a sequence of three podcasts hosted by this book's co-author, Robert J. Marks, at MindMatters.AI in 2019.

1. "Don't go towards the light!" https://mindmatters.ai/podcast/ep56/.

2. "Experiences of heaven," https://mindmatters.ai/podcast/ep57/.

3. "Biblical accounts of near-death experiences," https://mindmatters.ai/podcast /ep59/.

CPSIA information can be obtained
at www.ICGtesting.com
Printed in the USA
FSHW011439070421
80222FS